CANALS IN COLOUR

CANALS IN COLOUR

ANTHONY BURTON

Photography by Derek Pratt

BLANDFORD PRESS

LONDON

First published 1974
by Blandford Press Ltd,
167 High Holborn, London WC1V 6PH

ISBN 0 7137 0715 1

Colour plates by Colour Reproductions, Billericay
Printed in Great Britain by
Richard Clay (The Chaucer Press) Ltd,
Bungay, Suffolk

Contents

1 WHY CANALS?

What do canals mean to the average man or woman of today? Well, that depends very much upon the individual. For some, canals are convenient places for disposing of unwanted prams, rusty bicycles and old car tyres; for others they are unpleasantly dirty things that slide around the backsides of old industries and are best forgotten; for thousands of anglers they are simply a good source of fish; and for a very few they are a source of livelihood. Increasingly, though, for a growing number of people, they are a source of enjoyment and relaxation, settings for that marvellous pastime of messing about in boats. Two hundred years ago, however, canals were looked upon in a quite different way. To the people of the eighteenth century they were the marvels of the age, technological miracles, the carriers of wealth and plenty. It is difficult now, looking at a thin, spidery thread of water meandering away across the landscape, overshadowed perhaps by the rush and noise of a new motorway, to see an old canal as it must have appeared when it was brand new. But to appreciate canals to the full, it is worth making that effort to force one's imagination back through the years to see just how important canals once were to the development of Britain.

The middle of the eighteenth century saw the beginning of what we now call the Industrial Revolution. New inventions and new materials, new ways of organising the country's work force, the growth of towns based on factories and mills, all were combining to change Britain from a country of farmers and craftsmen to one dominated by industrialists. But among all the bustle and change, one aspect of life remained obstinately and dismally static. Transport in the middle of the century had hardly improved since medieval times, and it would not be unfair to say that the new industrialists would have much preferred the road system of Roman Britain to the system with which they had to cope every day.

The old high roads of Britain were wretched affairs. From the accounts left by travellers, it seems a marvel that anyone managed to move anywhere at all. In theory the maintenance of the highways was the responsibility of the individual parishes through which the road passed, and each able-bodied man was supposed to put in six days' work a year on road-mending, under the supervision of an elected surveyor. The workers were not the most willing of road repairers, as is clear from an account written by John Hawkins in 1763: 'The days for performing the Statute-Duty are so far from being considered as days of labour, that as well the farmers as the common day-labourers, have long been used to look on them as holidays, as a kind of recess from their accustomed labour, and devoted to idleness and its concomitant indulgences of Riot and Drunkenness.'

The surveyor who was supposed to be in charge was seldom of much help, for his appointment followed the 'Buggins' turn' principle, rather than any consideration of his merit or knowledge of roads. Small wonder that Hawkins described the whole affair as 'a contest between Ignorance armed with Authority on the one side and invincible Obstinacy on the other'. The authorities tried desperately to keep their roads from becoming totally impassable quagmires by issuing a series of laws forbidding the use of narrow-wheeled vehicles, but the laws were ignored and the roads continued to deteriorate. Daniel Defoe, who was a great traveller, described the road to Nottingham at the beginning of the century:

> You enter the deep clays, which are so surprisingly soft, that it is perfectly frightful to travellers, and it has been the wonder of foreigners, how, considering the great numbers of carriages which are continually passing with heavy loads, those ways have been made practicable; indeed the great number of horses every year kill'd by the excess of labour in those heavy ways, has been such a charge to the country, that new building of causeways, as the Romans did of old, seems to be a much easier expense.

The beginnings of improvements came when the old system gave way to a new era of road-building, with the introduction of the turnpikes. These new roads were mostly constructed with the aid of private finance, and users had to pay tolls. They were a major improvement and form the basis for our modern road network. But, at first, the differences were not sufficient to ensure that the needs of the country were met, for there were still no new road-building techniques. Travellers continued to spell out the horrendous conditions they met. Henry Skrine penned this account of a journey from Knowsley:

> I cannot find terms adequate to the idea I would convey of the wretched road between this place and Liverpool . . . The great road itself is unworthy of the name of turnpike, and a scandal to

> the town it approaches, being a continued series of unequal stones piled on one another, so as to form the roughest pavement in the universe. The infinity of carts and waggons that crowd it, form another inconvenience, as they are commonly driven by boys, and sometimes are without any conductor, so that a prudent traveller must be perpetually turning out of the way, into a miry summer track to avoid them.

Hardly an improvement over Defoe's roads.

But not all overland traffic used roads. A major part of the carrying trade followed the old pack-horse routes, often ways of great antiquity, which took a high-level route well clear of the cloying mud of the valleys. But strings of pack-horses are not suitable for moving heavy or bulky goods, so at the mid-century there was still no efficient and cheap way of moving goods overland.

The alternative was to move goods by water, along the rivers or around the coast. At the end of the century engineers worked out the relative efficiency of land and water transport. They found, after a series of experiments, that the average pack-horse load was one eighth of a ton, that a waggon pulled by one horse on an old soft road could carry five-eighths of a ton, and if placed on one of the new hard roads then being built by MacAdam, the load could be increased to two tons. Once goods were put on the water, however, a single horse towing a barge could shift a thirty-ton load.

Here was an obvious incentive to take cargoes off the roads and put them on to the rivers, but rivers, too, have disadvantages. Rocks, rapids, shallows and shoals, all can make navigation difficult if not impossible. To some extent these could be overcome by improving the navigation with artificial aids. To allow for the fall of the river, navigation weirs were introduced. In the simplest form, stout wooden beams were fixed across the river, the lowest resting on the river-bed, the highest above the level of flood water. The space between the beams was then spanned by vertical posts, called 'rimers', and the last gaps closed by movable wooden paddles. When boats wanted to pass, the paddles, rimers and top beams were removed and boats shot down on the flood of water that was released or were laboriously winched upstream against the torrent. This system was not only cumbersome, but, from all accounts, dangerous as well. The ultimate answer to this problem of changing level came with the introduction of the now familiar pound-lock.

The pound-lock plays such an important part in the development of

Elevation: Going 'down'

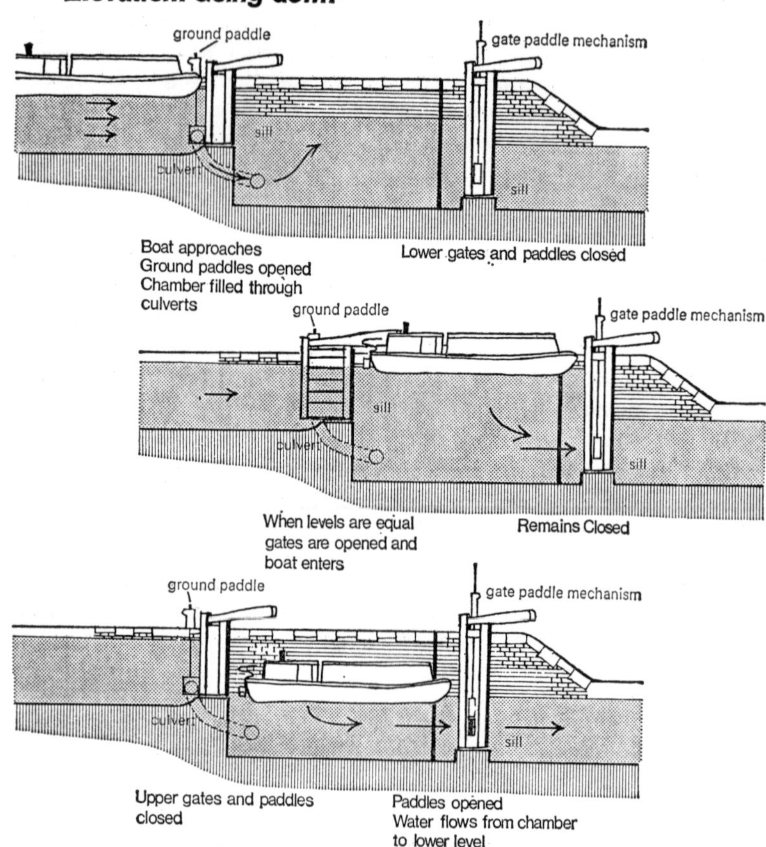

Plan: Lock filling

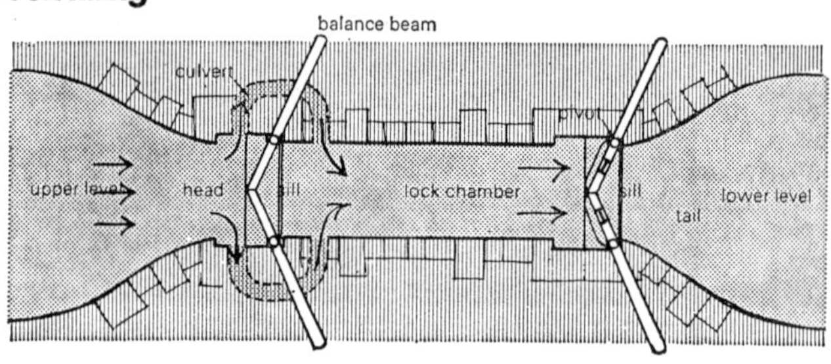

navigations and canals, that it is worth taking a moment to discuss it and how it works. In essence, the pound-lock, or lock as it is usually known, is a watertight chamber, usually made of brick or stone, built into the river or canal. It is closed at either end by massive gates which are kept tight shut by the pressure of the water against them. Water can be allowed into and out of the lock through either a hole cut into the gates on the uphill side or through a specially constructed culvert. In either case, the flow of water is controlled by movable paddles. Once the top paddles are opened, water can flow into the chamber until the levels are equal inside and out. Then the top gate can be opened and the boat floated into the lock. The paddles are then shut, and similar paddles opened at the lower end, so that water can flow out of the chamber and the boat steadily becomes lower within the lock. When the levels are again equal the bottom gates are opened and the boat can go on its way downstream. For a boat passing upstream, the process is simply reversed. The lock is one of those devices that are easier to understand from observation than from description. But, in essence, it provides a watery stairway to enable boats to cope with changes in level.

The earliest waterway to make use of a pound-lock was the Exeter Canal, a short cutting built in the 1560s to by-pass part of the River Exe. Other river improvements included the construction of artificial channels to by-pass particularly difficult sections, dredging, pile-driving to strengthen banks and the building of navigation weirs and locks. By the mid-eighteenth century river improvement had gone just about as far as possible. Busy commercial routes, such as the Aire and Calder Navigation in Yorkshire, had been opened and ambitious schemes such as the Kennet Navigation, joining Reading to Newbury, had been built. The Kennet Navigation was a remarkable example of just how far river improvement had been pushed, for its builders were faced with the problem of a river that dropped 2·1 m (7 ft) for each mile of length. To overcome this they had to build 18 locks in the 30 km (18½ miles) route.

But for all the engineers could do the heart of England was untouched, and in the central areas where the new industries were noisily demanding improved transport, the navigations offered no help—there was still no alternative to bad roads and slow expensive carriage. Also, the great rivers of the country were isolated one from another. To go from Trent to Mersey meant a long overland haul, to move from Thames to Severn, the same. One method was to send goods around the coast, but there the coastal shipping was prey to the notorious unreliability of the British weather: cargoes were locked up in ports as everyone sat around waiting for a favourable wind, and even when a ship set sail it could become becalmed or be blown into port again by a sudden storm. A famous case was quoted by Sir Edward Parry, who was arguing in favour of cutting a canal through the centre of Scotland: two boats left Newcastle on the same day, one bound for Bombay, the other taking the northern route to Liverpool—the Bombay boat was the first to arrive.

It was not surprising, given its obvious advantages, that business men and industrialists began talking about the possibility of bringing water transport to the whole country. But this would involve more than the improvement of existing rivers, it would involve the construction of brand new rivers, artificial waterways quite independent of the old routes. It would mean building canals. The idea was not new: on the Continent of Europe such great enterprises as the Canal du Midi were already proving their worth, but the British have always been an insular lot, and the eighteenth-century British were no exception. There was much talk, but for a long time nervousness about new ideas proved stronger than ambition. A British canal system to cover the country seemed a far-off dream.

2 BUILDING THE CANALS

Francis Egerton, third Duke of Bridgewater, was not the type of young man one would normally cast in the role of innovator for a vast new system of transport. In 1758 he was indistinguishable from many other young noblemen mixing in the fashionable world of London society, their Grand Tour behind them. He fell in love, exactly as a young nobleman should, but from that point the story turned from the familiar lines into quite a different narrative. The twenty-two-year-old Duke was very different from the popular image of an eighteenth-century aristocrat. Far from being a wit, a fop or even something of a rake, he was serious, sober and rather dourly puritanical. How he ever came to attach himself to the beautiful young Duchess of Hamilton, who was already the subject of a number of decidedly titillating rumours, must remain a mystery. But he did and, inevitably, they quarrelled. The young man quit society and made for his Lancashire estates and was said by the Earl of Ellesmere 'never to have spoken to another woman in the language of gallantry'.

Love's loss was the country's gain. The Duke threw himself energetically into the serious business of managing his various concerns, among which the coal mines of Worsley Delph, outside Manchester, featured prominently. He soon came across the problem that beset many another mine-owner at that time: the problem of getting the coal from mine to customer. In this case the main customers were in the nearby city. Other mine-owners in the district were benefiting from the recently opened Sankey Brook, a new river navigation, and could undersell the Duke. What was he to do? His first thought was to carry the coal to the nearby river Irwell by means of a short, artificial cut, but he found the owners of the Mersey and Irwell Navigation to be something less than reasonable. They believed they had the Duke just where they wanted him: he needed to send his coals *via* the Irwell, and they put up the prices to meet the situation. But the Duke had other ideas. He sat down with his agent, John Gilbert, and together they worked out a plan that would make them entirely independent of the old Navigation Company. They planned a canal that would run directly from the mines at Worsley to the heart of Manchester.

The first problem the Duke faced was the problem of obtaining permission to build such a canal, and that entailed the passing of a special Act of Parliament. Just as building a new road in the twentieth century arouses opposition from all kinds of people, and especially from those through whose neighbourhood the new road is planned to pass, planners of new canals were faced by vociferous opponents. Loudest and most voluble of the Duke's opponents were the Irwell Company, infuriated by this impudent upstart. But the old Company had been too greedy too often, and their prophecies of doom and ruination should a new canal be allowed to take away their trade went unheard. In 1759 an Act was passed authorising the Duke of Bridgewater to build his canal.

Authorisation was one thing, planning and building quite something else. The obvious starting point would have been to call in an engineer experienced in canal construction, but as such a work had never been attempted in Britain before, such an engineer simply did not exist. Instead the Duke and Gilbert called in a man who had a growing reputation for inventiveness and ingenuity, James Brindley. If a twenty-two-year-old Duke seems odd casting for the part of first canal promoter, then the appointment of an almost illiterate millwright as first engineer is even more bizarre. Brindley began his working life as an apprentice millwright, and from a very early age showed a mastery of his craft and a quite remarkable ability to solve complex problems in his head. Throughout his life he tackled problems by retiring to a dark room, where he would sit or lie thinking the problem through to a solution without the benefit of any written notes. He could view a complicated piece of machinery, then go away and later describe it in complete and accurate detail. His abilities soon raised him high in the ranks of his trade, but when he came to the Duke of Bridgewater the nearest he had come to canal construction was building an underground channel 550 m (600 yds) long as part of a drainage scheme at the Clifton mines.

What the unlikely trio lacked in experience, they made up for in enthusiasm and boldness. They determined on building a wide canal that would run straight out of the mines at one end, where the drainage would keep it supplied with water, and would then continue as a lock-free waterway into Manchester. One major obstacle lay in the way—the river Irwell that crossed the route. In avoiding this the boldness of the plan was apparent, for they planned to stride over the old rival by building an aqueduct at Barton.

Nothing of the sort had been seen in Britain, and even the Duke began to have misgivings about the practicality of the scheme. He called in one of the leading engineers of the time who inspected the plans, inspected the site by the Irwell and then remarked caustically that he had 'often heard of castles in the air, but never was before shown where any of them was to be built'. The young Duke, to his great credit, showed more faith in Brindley and Gilbert than in the expert, and the plans went forward.

The building of the canal caused a good deal of excitement and people came from all parts of the country to see the work in progress, to watch the great gangs of men hacking their way through the countryside and, above all, to see the work on the Barton aqueduct. What they did not see was the Duke's struggles to find the money to keep the work going. He had undertaken to finance the whole project from his personal funds, and though he was a rich man he found his resources stretched to the uttermost. He sold his London house, mortgaged everything mortgageable, borrowed from relations, obtained a bank loan and, in spite of all these efforts, still seemed unable to keep out of debt. Things became so bad that he even suffered the indignity of being pursued by a local creditor until he was finally cornered in one of his own barns. But somehow he kept going, the work went on until, in 1761, all was triumph. The Bridgewater Canal from Worsley to Salford was open for traffic.

Now the castle in the air had become a reality. Sightseers flocked to it, parties of fashionable ladies and gentlemen made special excursions, and no traveller would dream of writing of his journeys without including an account of the wonderful work at Barton. This letter, written to the *St James's Chronicle* in September 1763, perfectly catches the sense of awe and wonder felt by the writer:

> 'Tis not long since I viewed the artificial curiosities of London, and now have seen the natural wonders of the Peak; but none of them have given me so much pleasure as I now receive in surveying the Duke of Bridgewater's navigation in this county. His projector, the ingenious Mr Brindley, has indeed made such improvements in this way, as are truly astonishing. At Barton bridge he has erected a navigable canal in the air; for it is as high as the tops of trees. Whilst I was surveying it with a mixture of wonder and delight, four barges passed me in the space of about three minutes, two of them being chained together, and dragged by two horses, who went on the terras of the canal, whereon, I must own, I durst

> hardly venture to walk, as I almost trembled to behold the large river Irwell underneath me, across which this navigation is carried by a bridge, which contains upon it the canal of water, with the barges in it, drawn by horses, which walk upon the battlements of this extraordinary bridge.

Arthur Young put it somewhat more prosaically: 'The effect of coming at once on to *Barton Bridge*, and looking *down* upon a large river, with barges of great burthen towing along it; and *up* to another river, hung in the air, with barges sailing upon it, forms altogether a scenery somewhat like enchantment.'

Just as enchanting to many was the effect of the canal on the cost of coal. The waterway led deep underground, so that the coal could be loaded almost at the coal face and then carried to Salford, where its price dropped to exactly one half of what it had been before the opening of the canal. There were three lessons soon learned from the construction of the Bridgewater: first, that it was possible to construct a canal that would be entirely independent of any natural waterway, taking its own line across country; second, that if goods were carried by canal, their prices could be dramatically reduced; and last, but not least important for the future of canals, it soon became clear the canals could bring enormous profits to their owners, for the Duke was soon able to repay all his debts and begin to build a new fortune.

Once the lessons of the Bridgewater had been learned there was a great flurry of activity as new canal schemes were launched. A dozen of these came into being in the ten years after 1761, and they included some of the most important of all our canals. Acts were passed, for example, authorising the building of the Oxford Canal to link the Midlands to the Thames, the Leeds and Liverpool to cross the Pennines, the Birmingham at the very centre of the newly developing system, the Forth and Clyde in Scotland, and, most important of all, the first of the canals that were to form 'The Cross'. This last was a scheme to join together the four great rivers of England—Trent, Mersey, Thames and Severn. The Staffordshire and Worcester was approved in 1766 and the same year saw the passing of the Act for the Trent and Mersey or Grand Trunk Canal.

The new canal construction programme was organised on a very different basis from that of the Bridgewater Canal. It was clear that these new ambitious schemes could not be financed by single individuals, and companies were set up and the money raised by selling shares. The promoters of the new canals came mainly from among the ranks of the new class of industrialists—men such as the famous potter Josiah Wedgwood, who was the main promoter of the Trent and Mersey Canal. Wedgwood, his works situated in the centre of England, desperately needed a route to the sea so that he could bring in china clay from the quarries of the West Country. Equally, he also needed a way of carrying his delicate manufactured ware that did not involve bumping it around over bad roads or humping it in panniers on pack-horses. So convinced was he of the value of the canal to his business that he planned a grand new pottery on the banks of the Trent and Mersey, the Etruria Works, and, on the opposite bank, its lawns sloping down to the water, he built a new family home, Etruria Hall.

The new canal companies found themselves facing problems similar to those that had confronted the Duke of Bridgewater. The first was that of getting an act through Parliament. This was long, tedious and expensive and, as most of the manufacturing towns were unrepresented in Parliament, it also involved a great deal of lobbying. The opponents of canals came in various shapes and forms—those who simply did not want a canal at the bottom of the garden, old navigation companies that feared the growth of a powerful rival, mill-owners concerned about a threat to their own water-supplies. Each side issued reams of pamphlets arguing the rival cases, petitions for and against appeared, and it was not unknown to find the same signatures on both, and efforts were made to win the support of individual members of Lords and Commons. These efforts often involved thinly disguised bribery: this canal company might offer to supply free drainage to the mines on his lordship's estates, that navigation company might offer especially favourable terms to that MP's goods. 'Declaring an interest' was not a common practice in eighteenth-century parliaments. In the end, when all necessary pockets had been lined and sufficient outstretched palms greased, the company would receive its act authorising the construction of the canal.

Canal acts are interesting documents. They specify just how much capital may be raised. For example, 'The Company of the Proprietors of the Staffordshire and Worcestershire Canal Navigation' were empowered to raise £70,000, by selling shares of £100 each, and could raise a further £30,000 if it turned out to be needed. (One wonders just how much canal-building £100,000 would purchase today.) The company were also told how much they could charge traders who wished to use the canal. In this case it was 1½*d* (½p) per ton per 1 mile (1·6 km) 'for all Iron, Iron-stone, Coal, Stone, Timber and other Goods', although lime and limestone were cheaper to transport. Stone for road repairs and manure for farmers along the route were carried free 'provided such Articles pass through a Lock only when the Water flows over the Weir' or, in other words, when the canal was full. This last condition was important, for water-supply and conservation was and is a major problem for all canals. The Act also specified the route to be followed, which often turned out to be a compromise between the ideas of the engineers and the interests of local landowners, and there were clauses specifying which brooks and rivers could be tapped for water-supplies and which could not. Once all was agreed work could start.

One of the chief beneficiaries of the success of the Bridgewater Canal was James Brindley. He was no longer a mere millwright, nor even a canal engineer—he was *the* canal engineer. The praise heaped upon him was fulsome to the point of embarrassment: 'Many of his projects were of so stupendous kind, and so incomprehensible to vulgar minds, as to subject him to great ridicule, till the scoffers were put to confusion by their successful execution,' wrote Thomas Pennant in 1782, and William Bray wrote of 'Mr Brindley's genius, which broke out like the sun from a dark cloud'.

Brindley, in his role of Chief Engineer to most of the new companies, travelled throughout Britain planning the new canal routes. His reputation may have been enormous, but he was not an easy gentleman to handle. He appears to have been stubborn, ill-tempered and opinionated, and, having so many commitments, he was never able to devote as much time to any single project as his employers wished. Perhaps his greatest fault was that he was unwilling or unable to learn from others. No doubt the affair of the Barton aqueduct influenced him in this. The Duke had gone to the learned and educated who had pronounced the scheme fantastic and impossible; but the uneducated millwright had been proved right and the experts wrong. Thereafter Brindley relied on Brindley. The style of his canals is so personal that he could be said to have written his signature on the landscape of Britain, because James Brindley had certain set ideas about canal construction. His main concept was that canals should be kept on one level for as long as possible, using what we now call 'contour cutting'. This means that a Brindley canal seldom goes over or through an obstacle if there is any way of going round it, resulting in a delightful meander through peaceful countryside for today's pleasure boats and an agonising frustration of time-wasting for the old boatmen who were there for profit not fun.

The most important decision that Brindley took followed his work on the Bridgewater, when he tackled the problems of the Midlands canals. He had already begun an extension of the Bridgewater to the Mersey at Runcorn, where the canal was to be lowered to the level of the river by a set of locks, each 21·3 m (71 ft) long and 4·5 m (15 ft) wide. These locks were obviously thought to be too large, too wasteful of water, so Brindley solved the problem for his new canals by building locks to exactly one half that size, reducing the width to 2·2 m (7 ft 6 in). By that one decision he both set the standard for the country as a whole and vitally affected the long-term development of canals. Because the size of its locks determines the size of the boats that can use a canal, a special boat was developed to fit Brindley's locks, the now familiar narrow boat. It must have seemed a more than adequate craft at the time, with its load of thirty tons, but Brindley could not know that in less than a century railways would come, making such loads seem hopelessly inadequate.

However, the decision was taken, and Brindley trotted around the country on his old horse, surveying new works by what he called 'ochilor survey or a ricconitring'. It was a wearying life, constantly on the move, wanted everywhere and with seldom enough time to handle any job properly. He made a fortune, but in doing so he ruined his health. Wedgwood wrote to a friend in 1767: 'I am afraid he will do too much, & leave us before his vast designs are executed; he is so incessantly harassed on every side, that he hath no rest, either for his mind, or Body, & will not be prevailed upon to have proper care for his health.' The prophecy proved accurate. James Brindley died of diabetes in 1772, at the age of fifty-five, with his greatest work, the Trent and Mersey Canal, still unfinished.

The first decade of canal-building was entirely dominated by the figure of Brindley, who in so many ways led where others would follow. It was Brindley who planned the first canal tunnel, the Harecastle tunnel on the Trent and Mersey, more than 2·4 km (1½ miles) long. It received almost as much admiration as did the Barton aqueduct: 'Gentlemen come to view our eighth wonder of the world, the subterraneous navigation, which is cutting by the great Mr Brindley, who handles rocks as easily as you would plumb-pies, and makes the four elements subservient to his will.' That statement was more notable for its enthusiasm than for its accuracy, for Brindley's workmen met appalling difficulties in the excavation: they ran into quicksands, hard rock had to be hewn away or blasted out with gunpowder, and always there was the problem of water that seeped through the workings, and could only be kept at bay by the constant working of the primitive steam-engine that drove the pumps. Eleven years they sweated at Harecastle, driving their narrow, low and crooked channel through the hill, and the way was not open until 1777, five years after Brindley's death. Besides the main tunnel, 2649 m (2897 yd) long, there were numerous side channels cut to get at the coal they found in the hill. Though now disused, having been replaced by a second tunnel, it remains a remarkable piece of pioneering work.

Another of Brindley's contributions to canal construction was the development of 'puddling'. This entails mixing clay and water to a semi-fluid state and then stamping the sticky mess into the bed of the cut in successive layers until it forms a watertight layer. A foul and wearying job for the men who spent their days tramping up and down in the clinging mixture, but astonishingly effective.

These early years showed a number of trends and innovations that were to prove of great importance in the development of the canal system. For a start, a particular method of employing labour was established. The Duke of Bridgewater had hired workmen directly, but the new companies soon found this both a troublesome and an expensive business. It meant that the company had to supply all the necessary tools and equipment, and even though these were little more than picks, shovels and wheelbarrows, they all had to be paid for, and then men had to be paid to look after them to ensure they were not stolen, and more men had to tour the diggings collecting the tools together and arranging for them to be taken to different parts of the workings. Even so, things got lost, though the items that disappeared sometimes seem a little odd. In May 1769, for example, one of the workmen on the Coventry Canal was charged with stealing 'part of a plank'—alas there is no indication in the records as to which part he stole. Add to all that the troublesome business of looking for labourers, and it was soon obvious that it was much more efficient to farm out sections of the work to independent contractors and let them worry about such matters. This became the generally accepted method for building canals.

Some of the problems that were to face canal companies over the next half century or so also began to appear. The first of these was cash: schemes that began in a fine, rosy glow of optimism soon began to look less delightful as periods of recession followed periods of boom, and work on canals such as the Oxford was frequently held up, not because of engineering difficulties, but because of lack of funds. Another problem that soon appeared was the jealous and sometimes ludicrous rivalries between the new companies. Each was anxious that no rival would be in a position to take away trade or water from itself. When two canals were to make a junction, there was often almost endless bickering about where that junction was to be, leading to such incredible absurdities as the original junction between the Coventry and Oxford canals. Because the two companies could not agree, the routes actually ran side by side for well over a kilometre until they reached Longford. Many years passed before sanity prevailed and a new junction was made at Hawkesbury.

At the end of the 1770s there was a pause in canal building: the first great rush came to an end. The main reason was the recession caused when a minor military skirmish developed into the American War of Independence, a major conflict that involved other European powers and badly affected Britain's trade. Between 1780 and 1785 only two new canals were begun—the Thames and Severn and the Birmingham and Fazeley—and work on older canals, such as the Oxford and the Leeds and Liverpool was at a halt. Once the war was over, canal-building began again with a vengeance. In the early 1790s such a torrent of new canal schemes were put forward that these years came to be known as the years of Canal Mania. In 1790, one new Canal Act appeared on the Statute Books, there were six the next year and six more in 1792; but in 1793 no fewer than nineteen new Acts were approved, and many of these were for routes of major importance.

The mania years were so called not just because of the numbers of new canals that were planned, but because of the sudden scramble to invest in them. The first canals had been mainly financed by the men who stood to gain from their existence, those who needed the new transport. The shares they bought were all of high value—£200 each for the Trent and Mersey, £140 for the Birmingham. Though they might have bought their shares for the value of the canal, they soon found that they had made an investment that was appreciating at a staggering rate. The Birmingham shares went up to £370 by 1782 and ten years later they were changing hands for £1,170! Small wonder that speculators suddenly saw canals not as useful additions to a transport system, but as cornucopias pouring out an endless stream of steadily increasing profits and dividends. Shares were sold in much smaller denominations, sometimes as low as £1 each. As soon as news about the opening of a new subscription reached the general public, there was a stampede to get in at the first issue. The engineer, John Sutcliffe, wrote in 1816: 'It can be no matter of surprise, that the public mind should have been so much inflamed with canal speculations . . . and caused many, who were determined to become canal subscribers cheerfully to submit to sleep in barns and stables, when beds could not be procured in the public houses, where meetings were held to receive subscriptions for newly projected canals.'

The speculators in their mad dashes around the countryside often showed no discrimination and less sense. As far as they were concerned canals meant money and they wanted a part of it. There was no question of investigating each new scheme to see if it was practicable, to estimate whether the canal could ever show a profit, or indeed to see if it could be built at all. All canals were to be Birmingham canals, destined to make the lucky investor rich. Inevitably there were disappointments: some schemes never got started at all, others soon foundered with little to show for the money put in except a sad and empty ditch, yet others were completed but never yielded a profit. Canal companies formed in the 1790s, when optimism was at its height, found themselves faced with a problem with which we are still all too familiar—inflation. Costs worked out in 1790 could look terribly sick a decade later. The original estimates for the Kennet and Avon Canal suggested that it could be built for £400,000. The money was raised and duly spent, and the company had to return to Parliament for the authority to raise more. In the end, it cost more than a million pounds.

The speculators may have been frequently greedy and stupid, nevertheless they helped to finance many, many canals and establish a system of waterways across the face of Britain. These canals were of a different generation from the first canals of Brindley's days. The new engineers could draw on the experience of the old and, by making use of new techniques and new materials, they changed the style of canal-building. The old style of contour cutting, going around obstacles by a long and circuitous route, gave way gradually to the use of the new technique of 'cut and fill'. The essence of this is to cut deep into rising ground and then to use the excavated material to build up an embankment in the succeeding valley. In this way, canals could be made to take a much straighter, more direct route than had ever been possible before

The best way to see how canal construction changed over the years is to look at examples. The Act for the Ellesmere Canal was passed at the height of the canal mania in 1793. It was originally intended to join Shrewsbury to Chester, with various branches, including one main section to Ruabon, near Llangollen. The construction of the canal was supervised by two of the greatest of all canal engineers: William Jessop and Thomas Telford. Jessop was appointed as Chief Engineer and the development of the main line as we know it today must stand to his credit. The route begins at the Chester Canal, rising at once, by means of a steep flight of locks, by the side of Hurlestone reservoir. In the course of its route to Ruabon, every type of construction is met. There are examples of old-style contour cutting in the awkward, hilly country round Ellesmere, where the canal twists and turns in a way that Brindley himself might not have been ashamed to own. Over Whixall Moss, the canal is lifted on a high embankment and follows a dead straight route for about 3 km (2 miles) and near Chirk are deep cuttings, high banks, an aqueduct and a tunnel.

What marks this route out from all others, however, is the daring of the engineers who threw the great aqueduct across the Dee valley at Fron Cysyllte, and here Telford, the other engineer, must be mentioned. When work on the canal began, Telford was employed as 'General Agent, Surveyor, Engineer, Architect and Onlooker of the Works', which is an elaborate way of saying 'general dogsbody'. At that time he had no experience of canal construction, and it was his great good fortune to start under the tutelage of such a generous master as Jessop. Telford learned quickly, fast enough to be able to move at short notice to take over work on the Shrewsbury Canal when the Chief Engineer, Josiah Clowes, died in 1795. Here he was again fortunate, for he met the famous ironmasters, William and Joseph Reynolds, who were leading proprietors in the company. A small aqueduct was planned to cross the river Tern at Longdon, and Reynolds suggested that it might be possible to hold the water in a cast-iron trough instead of the traditional heavy masonry. Telford was enthusiastic and the aqueduct was successfully built. Armed with this experience, he went back to Jessop and the Ellesmere Canal.

Exactly who should take the credit for the design of the Pont Cysyllte aqueduct is the subject of controversy, but some facts can be safely set down. Telford had built in iron and was enthusiastic about using the new material; Jessop was chief engineer and all engineering decisions rested ultimately with him. Exactly how much each contributed to the final plans is conjecture, but, whoever was responsible, it was agreed to cross the Dee with an iron trough aqueduct supported on eighteen masonry piers. The whole structure is over 300 m (1000 ft) long and stands 36·5 m (120 ft) over the river. It was, and is, the greatest single work of civil engineering on the whole British canal system. When we see Brindley's aqueducts, we need to stretch our imaginations to see them as the marvels that they seemed to contemporaries. No such act of imagination is needed at Pont Cysyllte, which still arouses admiration and even awe. It is not just the aqueduct itself that tells us it is of the new age of construction: the huge embankments that bring the canal to it are, in their way, equally impressive reminders of just how far canal technology had progressed in a very short time.

Another canal where the advance of technology and change in attitudes can be clearly seen is the Oxford in its northern section. The original plans for the canal were Brindley's, but in the 1830s it was straightened and widened, and the two routes can be seen side by side, the old meandering away across the fields, the new heading straight to its destination. At Newbold-on-Avon the old tunnel, a low, narrow opening in the hillside by the church, is now abandoned and a shelter for cattle; the new is still in use, built high and wide and including the luxury of a tow-path. To turn from Brindley's canal to the new is like coming from a country lane to a dual carriageway.

Other engineers besides Jessop and Telford were busy by the end of the eighteenth century, and many added their own distinctive trademarks to canals and the landscape. John Rennie, for example, was not perhaps the greatest of engineers, but he was certainly the most elegant of stylists. The excellence of his designs for masonry work can be seen as clearly in small bridges as in such impressive aqueducts as the Dundas on the Kennet and Avon or the Lune on the Lancaster. Benjamin Outram was a fine canal engineer, but his special contribution was the construction of tramways which formed connections between the canals and sites such as quarries, mines or large industrial works. These tramways were made of iron rails set into stone blocks that acted as sleepers and were the precursors of the nineteenth-century railway system, thereby showing the astuteness of the Duke of Bridgewater, who prophesied that canals would do well enough if only they could keep clear of 'those damned tramroads'.

By 1830, there was somewhere in the region of five thousand kilometres of navigable waterways in Britain. The early dream of 'the cross' to unite the four rivers had been realised with the completion of the Grand Junction, now part of the Grand Union, which joined London to the Midlands. By then, too, a new development had appeared, the ship-canal. Two of these were authorised in 1793, one to join Gloucester to the Severn at Sharpness, and the short Crinan Canal which cut across the peninsula between Loch Fyne and the Sound of Jura to save boats the long sea passage around Kintyre. But these were comparatively insignificant when set against the Caledonian Canal. This ambitious waterway was planned to cut across the very centre of Scotland, from Fort William in the west to Inverness in the east, and to take large sea-going vessels that would otherwise be making the long and dangerous passage around the north coast. The poet Robert Southey visited the workings with his friend Telford, the canal's engineer. Among his descriptions is this of the scene at Fort Augustus in 1819, and it is clear that canal technology had come a very long way indeed since Brindley's time.

> Went before breakfast to look at the Locks, five together, of which three are finished, the fourth about half-built, the fifth not quite excavated. Such an extent of masonry, upon such a scale, I have never beheld, each of these locks being 180 feet [54·8 m] in length. It was a most impressive and remarkable scene. Men, horses and machines at work; digging, walling and puddling going on, men wheeling barrows, horses drawing stones along the railways. The great steam engine was at rest, having done its work. It threw out 160 hogs heads per minute [approximately 8000 gallons or 36,000 litres]; and two smaller engines (large ones they would have been considered anywhere else) were also needed while the excavation of the lower docks was going on; for they dug 24 feet [7·3 m] below the surface of water in the river, and the water filtered thro' open gravel. The dredging machine was in action, revolving round and round, and bringing up at every turn matter which had never before been brought up to the air and light. Its chimney poured forth volumes of black smoke, which there was no annoyance in beholding, because there was room enough for it in this wide clear atmosphere.

Moving to Loch Oich, he marvelled to find the canal cut 'forty feet [12·1 m] below the natural surface of the ground'.

The Caledonian might have been the beginning of a new age of canal-building, instead it turned out to be near the end of the old, for the railway age was about to take over. No major canal project interrupted the railways' domination until the construction of the Manchester Ship Canal in the 1890s. But although the age of canal construction lasted scarcely more than half a century from the time of the Bridgewater Canal, it provided many fine waterways and some splendid monuments to the engineering skills of the pioneers. There are the giant aqueducts, Pont Cysyllte, Lune, Avoncliff and Dundas on the Kennet and Avon, Outram's Marple aqueduct on the Peak Forest. There are the tunnels that came after Harecastle: Dudley tunnel, 2900 m (3172 yd) long, opening out into vast subterraneous caverns and recently reopened; Blisworth tunnel on the Grand Junction, 2794 m (3056 yd) long; Sapperton, now derelict on the Thames and Severn; and, longest of all at 4988 m (5456 yd), Standedge tunnel on the Huddersfield Canal. Later engineers added long flights of locks, watery steps up hillsides: at Tardebigge on the Worcester and Birmingham thirty locks are lined up together to tax the staying power of the boatman, and at Bingley on the Leeds and Liverpool, the flight is replaced by a 'staircase' of five locks, each lock emptying straight into the one below and altering the level by 18·2 m (sixty ft).

Engineers also introduced various mechanical devices for overcoming differences in level, of which the most common was the inclined plane. In most of these, the system worked by floating the boats into 'caissons', which were simply large wheeled tubs full of water that ran on rails laid against the hillside. The caissons were balanced so that as one tub went up, the other came down. They were introduced into Britain by the Reynolds brothers at Ketley in 1788, but the planes are no more, only the remains of tracks can be seen at various sites, such as Morwellham at the end of the Tavistock Canal in Devon, at Foxton in Leicestershire, or at Hay, now part of the open-air industrial museum at Ironbridge.

As well as the physical monuments of the age, there are the men whose names have lived on—the engineers, Brindley, Jessop, Telford, Rennie, Outram, Whitworth, Clowes and others. Although these are the names that have come down to us, there are thousands of men connected with the canals who have remained anonymous, scarcely more than statistics, but who all played their parts. To understand canals, it helps to have some idea of the work involved in constructing them and of the men who did it.

Today, in books such as this, it is a convenient shorthand to talk of Brindley's Oxford Canal, Jessop's Grand Junction, Rennie's Lancaster and so on, but in using the shorthand we are guilty of grossly underestimating the contribution of others. True, the chief engineers were immensely important: they were responsible for the overall plan of the canal, deciding what line it was to take, how enough water was to be secured, where locks, cuttings, embankments and so forth were to be built. But they rarely supervised detailed work or actual construction. Some, such as Telford, might take an interest in some particular aspect of design; in Telford's case the lock-cottages gave him a chance to realise his first frustrated ambition of becoming an architect. But a successful engineer would inevitably have more than one project in hand at any one time, so that the day-to-day supervision of work fell to another. This was the resident engineer, who no doubt must often have felt that the chief engineer got all the glory while he himself was left with all the work.

The main problem facing the resident engineer was trying to ensure that the dozens of individual contractors, spread over many miles of countryside, did the job they were supposed to do. Contractors were usually given a certain length of canal to construct at an agreed rate; once that was done, they could collect their cash and get on with the next contract. Their ideal was to get a job done quickly, have it approved and move on: the engineer's concern was to get a job done satisfactorily. The story of canal construction, if read from the documents of the canal companies, often seems more like a campaign between warring generals than an account of co-operation in construction. The voice of desperation can be heard clearly in a letter from Archibald Millar, Resident Engineer on the Lancaster Canal, to the big and important contractors, Pinkerton and Murray. He begins by complaining of the bad quality of the puddling, and orders that it should be repaired, but not 'in your own patching way'. The letter continues 'I only want to do what is fair and honest. Thus I must tell you that the time is now come if you do not conform to all my reasonable directions and instructions, I shall not certify to the Committee nor recommend their paying you One Shilling', and he ends, 'Pray with what face could I meet the General Meeting, and say (if asked) Gentlemen you have good work for your money, when I know the very contrary to be the fact.'

By the side of the resident engineer worked the company secretary, a man whose main qualification seems to have been endless patience, for it was to the hapless secretary that anyone and everyone with a complaint against the company eventually came. It was his lot to persuade unwilling landowners to part with their land with the minimum of fuss, without having to go through all the formalities of compulsory purchase; it was in his office that irate farmers appeared, shouting that the workmen had left gates open and cattle were spread over half the county; it was to him that contractors came to complain about workmen, and workmen about contractors. The administrative business of the canal all passed through his hands. The life of the secretary was not an enviable one.

Both engineers and secretaries had staff to assist them, but they were only a few. Beneath them, in turn, was the great army of men employed by the contractors, the men who dug the channel, built the bridges and aqueducts, and tunnelled through the hills. From their work on the navigations they got the name 'navigators', later shortened to the more familiar 'navvy'. The thousands of miles of canal were dug not by excavators and mechanical diggers, but by men using the simplest of tools and the strength of their arms. The story of canal-building belongs in good measure to the anonymous navvy.

To understand the navvy and his work, we have to go back again to the Bridgewater Canal and the beginning of construction. When the Duke built his canal he employed local labour, many of the men coming from his own estates or from his coal mines. Canal-building was little more than a temporary intrusion into their lives. But gradually, as the system moved from one in which the workers were employed directly to one in which they were paid by contractors, the navvies changed too. Instead of local men taking a turn at navvying, there was a growing number of 'professional' navvies, men who spent their lives in the diggings, migrants moving on to another canal as soon as one was finished. Inevitably they developed skills and strengths that gave them an immediate advantage over locally recruited labour. In 1780, the Rev. Stebbing Shaw found just such a situation when he went to see the work at the Greywell tunnel on the Basingstoke Canal: 'The contractor, agreeable to the request of the company of proprietors, gives the preference to all the natives who are desirous of this work, but such is the power of use over nature, that while these industrious poor are by all their efforts incapable of earning a sustenance, those who are brought from similar works, cheerfully obtain a comfortable support.'

By the time of the mania years, the navvy as an itinerant worker, travelling the length and breadth of the country, was well established. They came from all over Britain, driven by poverty, particularly agricultural workers, who were often among those in great need. Sir Frederick Morton Eden in *The State of the Poor*, published in 1797, described the conditions of many classes of workers. The farm workers of Devon, for example, were paid one shilling (5p) a day, and Eden wrote 'no labourer can, at present, maintain himself, wife, and two children on his earnings'. Some were in far worse condition, and the poverty in Scotland and Ireland was worst of all. The Scots, particularly the Highlanders, were still suffering from the aftermath of the disastrous campaign of '45 and the Irish were reduced to living conditions of almost unbelievable squalor, living in turf huts on the bogs and marshes, inadequately clothed and with the potato as the staple of their diet. It is not surprising that they came in their thousands to dig the canals, abandoning homes and families to wander the countryside. For, in comparison with what they had known before, canal work paid handsomely. A worker on the Lancaster Canal in the 1790s could earn 2*s* 2*d* (11p) a day—more than double the pay of the Devon farm worker—and a skilled man such as a mason could earn three shillings (15p), though it must be borne in mind that money values have changed so much, it is difficult to imagine 15p *ever* being a good wage.

Though these wage rates were comparatively high, it is as well to remember that they only seem high in comparison with so many other workers whose wages were insufficient to keep them above starvation level, and who had to rely on parish relief. And the navvies worked for their pay. An engineer writing at the time estimated that the average navvy could shift twelve cubic yards of earth in a day. To get an idea of what that means, measure out a patch of ground 1·8 m (6 ft) by 2·7 m (9 ft) and then decide if you could dig that to a depth of 1·8 m (6 ft) in one day.

Digging the first canals meant no more than shovelling the earth so that it could be wheeled away, but as engineers began to favour 'cut and fill', new techniques had to be found for getting the spoil out of the cuttings. In shallow cuttings this was achieved by laying planks against the sides, but that gave way in deep cuttings to the 'barrow runs'. Planks were still laid up the steep slopes, but the barrows were hauled up by horses. The navvy had to walk up the plank, which was slimy with mud and clay, keeping the barrow steady in front of him. A sudden change in the horse's pace, or a slip on the plank, and down went the navvy, sliding to the bottom of the bank, barrow and mud tumbling after him.

The navvy's work was rough and he lived rough: home often meant nothing more than an improvised shelter or a turf hut, something that could be abandoned as soon as he was ready to move on. And life was rough in another sense. The navvy soon earned a fearsome reputation for fighting, drunkenness and rioting—a reputation of which he was by no means ashamed. So famous did the navvies become that work was actually held up on the Lancaster Canal in 1796 because the men had been hired by one of the parties in that year's election 'for no other purpose than to riot and do mischief'. Sometimes a navvy riot could be a serious matter indeed, battles could last for days and were only quelled by the military, sometimes with the loss of life. A riot at Barrow-on-Soar in Leicestershire in 1795 'among that newly-created, and so wantonly multiplied, set of men, the diggers and conductors of navigations' as the *Gentleman's Magazine* described them, ended with the troops opening fire: three rioters were killed outright and eight seriously wounded. It is hardly surprising that residents in small, isolated communities, where strangers were virtually unknown, were often terrified at the thought of hundreds of navvies suddenly descending on the district.

If we could go back to the end of the eighteenth century to look down on a canal digging we would be impressed by the epic scale of it all—the hundreds and thousands of men, the activity and industry. To contemporary observers, to whom such scenes were completely new, a tour of the operation brought wonder, astonishment and a bewildering variety of things to see. Perhaps they would start with a section of straightforward cutting—a long ditch, a scar in the landscape, where sweating men worked furiously filling the procession of barrows. Round them the earth would be churned by horses and carts, removing the debris or bringing tools and equipment. Along the route masons and bricklayers might be at work, constructing bridges to reunite the different parts of a farmer's land, severed by the new canal, or to carry a local road over the cutting. Further along a lock chamber might have been excavated and bricklayers would be at work lining the chamber, while carpenters prepared the massive lock gates. Beyond the lock, the canal might be going into a deep cutting: stretching to the horizon would be the steadily plodding rows of horses led by young boys, hauling the barrows up the runs, while the men far below seem no more than diminutive, scurrying figures on the bed of the cutting. Here the scene would be even busier, as the material from the cutting is loaded up to be carted away to an embankment on another part of the canal.

In the distance the visitor might see columns of thick, black smoke marking the place where bricks, made of the clay dug from the hill, are being fired, or he might find men at work in a newly excavated stone quarry. Visiting another section he might find few signs of activity: only a hill topped by large circular drums turned by horses treading endless circles around the frame. These are the horse whims, used to wind material up or down shafts sunk deep into the hill, to the men tunnelling far below. Occasionally the ground would shake as more rock is blasted by the tunnellers. If he went down to the tunnel mouth, the visitor would probably see waggon loads of earth and rock being pushed out along a specially laid track, and, if he were brave enough to go into the tunnel itself, he would find a scene that could have been described by Dante. In the darkness, lit only by the flickering light of candles stuck on the hats of the tunnellers, he would see the almost naked men hacking at the rock, and everywhere he would feel the threat of water, turning the floor to thick mud and dripping endlessly from the roof of the cavern. On an important canal he might also see an aqueduct being constructed. In the bed of a river piles would be driven to create a coffer-dam, behind which the men could work at the foundations of the piers. A small steam-engine might be working nearby, powering the pumps that would keep the space behind the dam reasonably dry. Finally, the visitor might go some distance from the canal to see the vast new reservoir being constructed to keep it supplied with water.

Scenes such as this marked the great canal-building period. This was the effort and energy that went into the peaceful waterways we enjoy today. Nothing like it had been seen in Britain since the Romans had built their towns, roads and huge defensive walls. When all was completed the canal could at last be opened. A fine procession of boats, loaded with the proprietors, company officials and local dignitaries, and with military bands playing patriotic airs, would set off down the waterway. Banners were flown, oxen roasted, toasts were drunk and unwary revellers fell into the canal. Guns were fired in salute, and before the day ended there was always someone ready with a song for the occasion.

All hail this grand day when with gay colours flying
The barges are seen on the current to glide,
When with fond emulation all parties are vying,
To make our Canal of Old England the pride.

The junketings over, the canal was officially open for trade.

3 THE CANAL IN USE

A mythology has grown up around the working life of the canals. Most people who know anything at all about the subject can give some sort of a description of the narrow boat and the boat family. The vessel itself is 21 m (70 ft) long with a cabin at the back, decorated with brightly coloured patterns and pictures of Carpathian castles, and on the cabin roof are the water jugs and other objects, painted with traditional rose designs. The whole family work the boat, which is pulled by the steady, reliable old canal horse. It is always a picture of Arcadia and innocence —and it never rains. Of course it is not entirely myth, but at best it represents only a small part of the canal story. For a start, the roses and castles decoration does not appear to have been used until the second half of the nineteenth century—the distinguished canal historian, L. T. C. Rolt, states that he has found no reference to it before 1875. Next, the narrow boat is only one type of many using the canals, and narrow boats themselves often ran on short journeys so that many boatmen lived on land. Even where the boat and its family did exist, reality often fell some way short of the ideal. Arnold Bennett, who knew the Trent and Mersey in its passage through the Potteries, wrote this description at the beginning of *Clayhanger*:

> It was a breezy Friday in July 1872. The canal, which ran north and south, reflected a blue and white sky. Towards the bridge from the north came a long narrow canal-boat roofed with tarpaulins; and towards the bridge from the south came a similar craft, sluggishly creeping. The towing-path was a morass of sticky brown mud, for in the way of rain that year was breaking the records of a century and a half. Thirty yards [27 m] in front of each boat an unhappy skeleton of a horse floundered its best in the quagmire. The honest endeavour of one of the animals received a frequent tonic from a bare-legged girl of seven who heartily curled a whip about its crooked large-jointed legs. The ragged and filthy child danced in the rich mud round the horse's flanks with the simple joy of one who had been rewarded for good behaviour by the unrestricted use of a whip for the first time.

In order to begin disentangling fact from fiction, we shall take a look at the development of the canal boat and its trade.

The earliest boats in use were the 'starvationers' of the Bridgewater Canal—crudely constructed narrow boats, that were little more than hulls. They had no need to be elaborate: there was no cabin for they were never taken on long journeys, and there was certainly no decoration. These, with the addition of a simple cabin, could be taken as the model for the 'Joey boats' that worked on the short, day runs in the Midlands. On the old river navigations, most boats were bow-hauled, that is the heavy barges were pulled along by teams of men, but on the canals towing was, from the first, the work of horses or mules.

There was little that was romantic about the first canal boats. They plied to and fro carrying bulk commodities, with coal being far and away the most important cargo. Looking through the account books of the Oxford Canal Company, for example, for the 1790s, one finds that, on average, tolls from coal carrying regularly account for two-thirds of the total collected for all goods.

But even in those early days another aspect of canal travel began to appear—passenger transport. The packet-boats offered quick, reliable transport, mercifully free from the jolts and bumps, not to mention the highwaymen, that afflicted the coach traveller. The Duke of Bridgewater seems to have been the first to operate such a service and, from this account in the *Annual Register* for 1774, trips on the Duke's boats could be rather jolly affairs: 'The Duke of Bridgewater has just built two packet-boats, which are every day towed from Manchester to Warrington; one carries six score passengers, the other eighty: Each boat has a coffee-room at the head, from whence wines, &c. are sold out by the Captain's wife. Next to this is the first cabbin, which is 2*s* 6*d* [12½p] the second cabbin is 1*s* 6*d* [7½p] and the third cabbin 1*s*[5p] for the voyage upon the canal.'

The packet-boats had priority over all other craft on the canal, and it is not difficult to imagine how important this order of precedence was, nor how difficult to maintain. Canals were only provided with a tow-path on one bank, so that boats passing in opposite directions or over-taking always ran the risk of ending up in a tangle of tow-ropes. The Bridgewater packets had few worries on this score, for on their bows they flaunted sharp knives, a reminder that they were prepared to slice their way through if necessary.

What is perhaps rather surprising is to find that as early as the eighteenth century people were taking pleasure trips on the canal.

Torchlight processions of boats made visits to Harecastle tunnel in the 1770s and, according to the Rev. Shaw, they sometimes took 'a band of musick', though if the band actually played in that narrow tunnel the cacophony must have been truly dreadful.

By the end of the eighteenth century, boats were carrying for long distances and already there was a good deal of variety among the different craft. On the Leeds and Liverpool, boats were 18·8 m (62 ft) long with a 4·3 m (14 ft 3 in) beam, and on the Welsh canals there were boats midway between these wide barges and the Midlands narrow boats—on the Neath Canal, for example, boats were 18·2 m (60 ft) by 2·7 m (9 ft). Then there were the tub-boats, such as those found on the Shropshire Tub-boat Canal or on the Bude Canal in Cornwall: these were exactly what their name suggests, floating oblong tubs that could be towed along in convoys of as many as twenty at a time. By the beginning of the nineteenth century there was a great variety of boats, and a great variety of boat owners.

Canal companies very rarely ran their own boats. They were content to collect tolls from other users, although this changed when railway competition grew and many companies tried the carrying trade themselves in an attempt to boost flagging profits. Large industrial concerns often ran their own fleets, and made major investments in improving the transport system. The famous Dowlais Iron Company of South Wales ran boats on the Glamorgan Canal, and to improve the connections they built many miles of tramway, even taking rails as far as the Brecon and Abergavenny Canal. Not all their schemes were completely successful. In 1815 a tramway bridge on the Penydarran tramway—the same tramway on which Trevithick conducted his steam locomotive experiments—collapsed while a train was crossing. The horse was killed, two men seriously injured and the waggons of iron fell into the river. Nevertheless, the Dowlais Company regarded the canal and its tramways as their major transport system, sending thousands of tons of cargo every week.

Among the newcomers to the transport scene were a number of carrying companies. One of these had already established a business carrying goods by land, and in the 1790s it began operating a fleet of canal boats. This was Pickfords, who remain today, after two centuries in the business, one of Britain's most important carriers. They ran both stage-boats and fly-boats. The first carried heavy goods, stopping overnight and then continuing the journey the next day; the latter were the canal expresses running with relays of horses and men, working both day and night. In this advertisement from a Birmingham paper of 1814, Pickfords describe the services they offered:

> Messrs Pickford beg leave to inform their Friends and the Public in general, that they have established a Pair of FLY STAGE BOATS weekly from hence to Leicester, and intermediate Places, which load goods at Birmingham every Thursday afternoon, Warwick every Friday, Banbury and Oxford every Saturday; and discharge at Market Harborough and Leicester every Monday, return from Leicester every Monday evening; discharge Warwick goods every Wednesday; and Birmingham every Thursday morning.
> By these Boats Goods are regularly conveyed to and from all Wharfs and Places on the Line of the Birmingham, Warwick and Napton, and Oxford Canals.
> An Arrangement is making, and will soon be completed (of which timely Notice will be given) for extra Boats to leave Birmingham every Tuesday.

RATES TO LEICESTER.	Light Goods	2/6*d* [12½p] per Cwt
	Heavy ditto	2/3*d* [11p] ditto
	Tyre, Iron and Nails	2/0*d* [10p] ditto

Another important group of boat-owners were the 'number ones'. They were the owner-boatmen who are the basis of most of the romantic stories of the canals. They owned their own boats, ran their own boats and lived on their own boats. They were the men and women who, to their own deep disgust, also came to be known as 'water gypsies'.

Relationships between the companies who owned the canals and the boatmen who used them were often, to say the least, strained. Just as companies had found that their interests and those of the contractors who took on the building work were often divergent, so, too, they found that owners and users had quite different priorities. The company wanted a nice, orderly, well-run canal, where every effort was made to conserve water, where tolls could be collected easily and accurately. The boatmen, however, wanted to get from start to destination in the quickest possible time, had little or no interest in the regulations optimistically formulated by the companies, and fiddled tolls when they thought they could get away with it.

The lock-cottages that still stand beside so many locks are reminders of the role played by the lock-keepers in trying to ensure the efficient running of the canal. The keepers were not there to work the locks: then, as now, that was the job of the boatmen. They were there to prevent water wastage, to prevent damage and to ensure that boats entitled to priority got it. They had a trying time. The present occupant of a lock-cottage on the Leeds and Liverpool Canal, who himself began work on the canal in the First World War, tells of one lock-keeper he remembers who waged constant war with the boatmen. This gentleman's particular hate was the boatmen who sneaked through his locks in the dark and left paddles open. He rigged up a special alarm system between locks and cottage, but the wily boatmen soon had the system beaten, and encouraged local lads to push the gates open at all hours of the night so that the keeper would come rushing out to find only an empty lock and not a boat in sight. The alarm system was abandoned.

Letters in the Dowlais Iron Company's records give an idea of the battle between company and boatmen. George Forrest, agent for the Glamorgan Canal, sent this letter of complaint about a boatman, William Meredith:

> I scarcely know one Boatman so *determinedly bad in his Conduct on the Canal*, in the present instance he on Saturday last wilfully stopped at the Canal at the Treble Locks (*where the greatest obstacle on the line already exists*) for more than an hour and a half, without any pretext whatever of misunderstanding or any thing of the kind, but because he *would* wilfully & knowingly force his Boat into the lock before his turn, and afterwards having gone with his Boat three miles [4·8 km] higher up the Canal he then left it to the sole Care of a little Child (his Brother) who true to the example set him, when told by the lock-keeper to stop the Boat till his brother returned, only cursed him & went on in spite of all remonstrances and it was only when I came up with him on my return from Cardiff that this embryo Villain would stop.

Toll collection was another headache for the companies, for tolls supplied their revenue. Tolls were payable at so much per ton per mile, the actual rate varying with the type of goods carried. The system first used was to rely on way-bills, giving details of the carrier's journey and the quantity and type of cargo. Experience soon showed, however, that way-bills could as often be classified as works of fiction as documents of fact. The companies needed a check of their own, so they introduced weighing and gauging. Each boat was taken to the company's docks and the distance from gunwale to water level measured with the boat empty, weights were then added and the distance again measured for each additional weight. The results were entered into a log book, and armed with this information a company official could always and easily calculate the weight of cargo carried by measuring the height of the gunwales above water.

The introduction of gauging greatly reduced the risk of cargoes being allowed to pass with incorrect way-bills as far as weight was concerned, but that did not end the possibilities of cheating. As rates varied for different cargoes, the boatmen occasionally tried to load their boats with cheap cargoes on top, covering the more expensive underneath, and would then try and get the lot past the toll collector at the cheap rate. Sometimes they were caught, as this warning poster put out by the Coventry Canal Company indicates:

> On FRIDAY, the 17th day of MAY inst, HENRY WOODWARD, the Steerer of a Boat, was brought before the County Magistrates, at Coventry, charged with endeavouring to EVADE THE TOLL payable to the COVENTRY CANAL COMPANY, In respect of several cases of Pipes which he had secreted in his Boat laden with Road Stone, on the 1st instant, and was CONVICTED of the offence, and fined in the mitigated Penalty of 1*s* [5p], and £1 0*s* 6*d* [£1·02½] expenses.

Myles Pennington, in *Railways and Other Ways*, looked back on a childhood spent on the Leeds and Liverpool Canal in the 1830s, and tells some even more alarming stories of the boatmen of the time: 'It was difficult to keep up an honest crew of men long: outside harpies were always on the lookout to tempt them. In one case a shop was opened at Wigan for the sale of stolen goods.' The main trouble, according to Pennington, was drunkenness: 'boatmen had a knack of taking out a gallon of rum from a hogshead and replacing it with a gallon of water, and they were not over particular as to the kind of water they put in.'

The reputation of the boatmen was so unsavoury that a Society was set up in the early nineteenth century with the aim of converting them to a more religious view of life. A chapel was established at Paddington and a magazine, *The Canal Boatman's Magazine*, started publication in 1829. The Society clearly did not intend to convert through flattery, witness this piece from the first issue:

> They are a class of men among whom ignorance prevails to a very great extent; and this is not to be wondered at, when it is considered that no adequate efforts have been made to afford instruction to them. Brought up from childhood to manhood without education in many instances, and from the nature of their employ-

ment separated from society, they have naturally imbibed principles and habits in direct opposition to the Bible; and having lived year after year in a dark and benighted state, they have attained to such careless and dissolute practices—such impiety, and decided wickedness, that it requires no small degree of confidence, to endeavour, in the strength of the Lord, to convert them from the error of their ways.

To this catalogue of evil, the writer added that they were prone to Sabbath-breaking, drunkenness, swearing and other sins, ending that they show a 'profligacy and demoralization truly awful'. The whole magazine abounds with lurid anecdotes of boatmen's behaviour, such as the story of Mr Attlebury, a boatman whom the police attempted to arrest for maltreating his horse. Other boatmen joined in the fight which ended with one police sergeant being wounded in the face by a boat-hook and all the constables in the canal. The Society was short-lived.

It would be wrong to assume that all canal boatmen were little better than a band of brigands. Newspapers and magazines publish stories of crime and fighting which they think will interest readers—stories of men going quietly about their work are not news. It is as well to bear this in mind when looking back through the records.

It often seems to a holidaymaker, cruising along the canals today, that the boatman's life must have been idyllic. It was nothing of the sort: the work was hard and the hours long. The charge that the boatmen were 'sabbath breakers' was true enough, since, particularly when the railways threatened their trade, they were forced to work a seven-day week. Boatmen would often be up at four or five in the morning and would keep going to eight or nine at night. The day started with feeding and harnessing the horse, then they were under way until progress was stopped at the first lock. If they were working a pair of boats, the second boat had to be bow-hauled through the lock. Working in this way, they could cover some twenty-five miles a day. But locks were not the only obstacles facing the boatmen, there were also tunnels to be negotiated. The early tunnels had no tow-paths, so the horse had to be unhitched and led over the top of the hill, while the boats were 'legged' through the tunnel. To do this, the boatmen put out boards that projected from the sides of the boat. They then lay on their backs on the boards, pressed their feet against the sides of the tunnel and walked the boat through. The strain of legging through long tunnels was considerable and at some, such as Blisworth, there were professional leggers to do the job.

On later canals tow-paths were often provided, as in the new tunnel built by Telford parallel to Brindley's old tunnel at Harecastle.

Quite early in the history of canals, engineers began to look for alternatives to the horse as a means of moving canal boats. The first experiments in using steam-power for boats took place not in Britain but in France. Experiments began, unsuccessfully, on the Seine in 1775. But, in 1783, the Marquis Jouffroy d'Abbans successfully travelled a section of the River Saône near Lyons in a 182-ton paddle-steamer, the *Pyroscaphe*. Five years later the first successful British steamboat was built by William Symington and ran on a lake near Dumfries. Robert Burns was among the party on the first trip.

British engineers were hampered by James Watt's patents covering the use of steam-engines, but following Symington's success, boats were built using the older type of engine—the Newcomen or atmospheric engine. In 1793, a successful run was made with a steamboat on the Sankey Brook and, always in the forefront of canal pioneering, a boat was commissioned by the Duke of Bridgewater and built by the American engineer, Robert Fulton. It was not a great success. Far more successful was the stern-wheeled steam tug, *Charlotte Dundas*, built by Symington for use on the Forth and Clyde Canal. In a trial in March 1802, she pulled a total weight of seventy tons for 31 km (19½ miles) in six hours against a strong head wind. The return journey was notably faster. But the boat created a considerable wash and as it was feared that it would cause damage to the banks, *Charlotte Dundas* was laid up.

The steamboat had to wait half a century before it came into regular use on the canals as anything but a tug. The horse remained the main source of power. Now that horse and tow-rope are hardly to be seen on the canals we are left with little more than the evidence of their passing, but much does remain to remind us of the busiest commercial period of the canals. We still have many canal-side warehouses, some of which have canopies over the water so that boats could be loaded under cover and some, more sophisticated, are actually built out over the water so that boats could float straight under the archways. The most famous examples of the latter type of warehouse were those built by Telford at Ellesmere Port, where the Shropshire Union joins the river Mersey, but these were, alas, destroyed quite recently. Other, if less impressive, examples do remain: Pickfords, for example, had such a warehouse at Worksop on the Chesterfield Canal and there is a splendid group at Sowerby Bridge, where the Rochdale Canal joins the Calder. Lock-cottages and tollhouses played important roles in the days of bustling commerce, and there are, of course, reminders of the horse-boats in the many inns and stables.

To see the traces of the old days at their clearest it is best to study the detail, the small scale. Look at almost any old canal bridge and there will be grooves cut deep into brick or stone or even, if one is still in place, into the iron guard plate. These are the marks scored by countless thousands of tow-ropes. Often, too, one can see the special arrangements that had to be made for the horse-drawn boats. Sometimes, near flights of locks where the horse would be unhitched, are bridges with two arches, one for the boat and a special tunnel for the horse. Sometimes, the reminders can be some distance from the canal itself—names such as 'Boat Horse Lane' survive near tunnels and mark the route over which the horse was led, while sweating boatmen legged the boat through beneath their hooves.

Among the most fascinating reminders of the horse-drawn boats are the different devices resorted to by the builders to cope with the problem that arose when they had to move the tow-path from one side of the canal to the other. Clearly the horse could not simply walk across a bridge, dragging the boat behind it, so special 'turn-over' bridges had to be designed. The simplest sort are constructed like ordinary bridges, but with a much wider span and long approach ramps: the horse walks up the ramp, down the other side so that it is facing the direction from which it came and then it doubles back under the bridge. That way the tow-rope does not have to pass over the arch. A much more elegant solution can be found in the 'snake' bridges. The principle is the same, but instead of long straight ramps, one ramp curls right round on itself to end beneath the arch. The most famous examples—and they are among the most beautiful of all canal structures—can be found on the Macclesfield Canal. Another ingenious solution to the tow-rope problem can be seen on the Stratford-on-Avon Canal, where metal bridges have a split down the centre to allow the rope to pass through rather than over.

We tend to look back on the great days of the horse-drawn boat through the rosy glasses of nostalgia. Even when we know that life on the canals was not all sweetness and light, it is all but impossible for the canal enthusiast not to take a romantic view of the age. But it is not only the present-day enthusiasts who cast wistful backward glances, canal company proprietors, too, dreamed of the old days of hectic trade and fat profits that preceded the fateful time when the railways came to Britain.

4 DECLINE AND RECOVERY

In the story of Britain's canals, the railway company has traditionally been cast in the role of wicked uncle; but the villain does not deserve all the boos and hisses in this particular melodrama. Certainly, railway competition profoundly affected the prosperity of the canals, but their eventual decline was due in no small part to the stupidity and greed of many of the canal-owners themselves. Had the companies begun by co-operating with each other, it might have been possible for the canals to offer an effective alternative to the railways, but the companies did not co-operate. Each pursued what it saw to be its own interests, with frequently disastrous consequences.

A classic example of non-co-operation can be found in the construction of the Grand Junction Canal to join London and the Midlands. It was quite obvious that it had an existing rival in the route via the Oxford Canal and the Thames, but it was equally obvious that the newcomer had the greater potential. The Grand Junction was to cut 103 km (64 miles) off the Birmingham to London route, and was to have broad locks instead of the narrow locks of Brindley's old route. It represented an improvement in every way. The Oxford Company, not surprisingly, were scared stiff at the thought of the revenue they would lose. Cleverly, they managed to get a clause inserted into the Grand Junction Act specifying that if tolls on the Oxford fell below £5000 a year the difference would be made up by the new Company, and after 1 January 1804, the level was to be raised to £10,000. That was fair enough as far as the Oxford was concerned, although the new Company may not have been too keen. What followed, however, was considerably less reasonable. To link the Grand Junction with Birmingham, it was planned to extend the Warwick and Birmingham southwards to meet it at Braunston, where the Grand Junction also met the Oxford. But now the special interests began to have their say. First, the Oxford Company insisted that the junction with the Warwick and Birmingham should not be at Braunston but at Napton, which meant that boats would have to travel 8 km (5 miles) of Oxford Canal between Braunston and Napton and pay tolls to the Oxford Company. Then the Birmingham interests had their say: insisting that the canal down to Napton should not be built with the new broad locks of the Grand Junction but with the old narrow type, thus ensuring that traffic would continue to come to Birmingham boats. The chance of building a direct, broad canal from London to Birmingham was lost, and ultimately everyone was the loser.

So busy were the canal companies in competing with each other that they were in no shape to compete with the much greater threat posed by the railways, following the opening of the Liverpool and Manchester Railway in 1830. How ironical it was that the first important main-line route should follow so closely the route of the first canal!

In the early days the railways offered no threat to the bulk-carrying trade which formed the major part of canal traffic, but they at once had a serious effect on the passenger trade. The canals could not hope to compete, and this gave the railways an immediate advantage when they began to take away the goods trade as well: the canals had to rely entirely on revenue from goods, the railways could spread costs over goods and passenger traffic. The canal companies began to fight back. In the past they had been content to act solely as toll-collectors, but now they began to run their own fleets, and tolls were reduced in an attempt to attract trade. But the real trouble lay elsewhere. The canal companies were inefficient, and the old narrow locks which had seemed adequate in the 1760s looked less so in the railway age. The canals had prospered, in part, from the complacency of the old river navigation companies and road-owners, who had been content to collect revenue without bothering overmuch about repairs and improvements. Now the canal companies discovered that they had made the same mistake. Improvements were put in hand. On some routes, such as the Trent and Mersey and the northern part of the Oxford, locks were duplicated and sections straightened to speed traffic. In an attempt to reduce the administrative problems of the old complex network, companies amalgamated. One such group, formed by the joining of the Birmingham and Liverpool Junction, the Ellesmere and the Chester, obtained permission to construct their own railway, and had a new lease of life as the Shropshire Union Railway and Canal Company. But it was all too late. Traffic was being taken off the boats and put into railway waggons. Whereas once industrialists had selected factory sites on the banks of canals, now they built by the new railways instead.

Railway dominance led many companies to sell out to the railways. Shareholders seeing their company trying unsuccessfully to compete with the local railway company were usually willing enough to accept any reasonable offer. Once they had gained control, the railway companies had little incentive to bother unduly with their canals. The system ossified: new routes were virtually unknown, improvements were few.

The influence of the railways was not all bad, though the attitude of many could be summed up by Clough's well known lines:

Thou shalt not kill; but needst not strive
Officiously to keep alive.

Some companies were more mindful of their obligations than others, and in this period many canals did continue to thrive. The short hauls of coal on the Birmingham system, for example, continued to be profitable. But the overall picture was one of decline, and there were few signs in the middle of the nineteenth century that anyone would ever again come forward to invest money in inland waterways. There were also many examples of railway companies actively hindering progress. In the mid-century there was a revival of interest in steam tugs. In 1856 the Moira Colliery bought a steam tug, *Pioneer*, which they intended to run on the lock-free Ashby Canal. This, however, was owned by the Midland Railway Company who were not in the least attracted to such a scheme and banned the tug, claiming that the wash and turbulence from the propeller would damage the banks. The Colliery refused to accept the decision and took the matter to court. Experiments were conducted, and the judges decided that no harm was done if the speed of the boat was kept down to 4·8 km (3 miles) an hour. Steam was back on the canal.

By the end of the nineteenth century there were fleets of steamers working the canals. One large fleet was owned and run by the Leeds and Liverpool Company and a second, probably the most famous of all carrying fleets, was run on the Grand Junction by Fellows, Morton and Clayton. These boats were standard pairs of narrow boats, except that a steam-engine was built into the first, which then towed the second boat, or 'butty', behind. They must have been an extraordinary sight. They worked as fly-boats, running day and night, and were kept so immaculately clean that the seven-man crew were dressed in brilliant white uniforms. Although the work was hard it was well paid, and more than one crewman managed to save enough to leave the fleet to buy a boat of his own, and set up in business as a number one.

The trouble with the steamers was the amount of space taken up by the engine. As the size of the boat was still limited by the size of the lock, the space could only be obtained by sacrificing cargo. To put in a steam-engine meant the loss of ten tons of cargo, and it was this as much as cost that kept the horse-drawn boat in use.

Later, in the twentieth century, the steam-engine was replaced by the much more compact diesel-engine. Even so, the horse continued to be used by canal boatmen right up to the present day. The profits a number one could make were always slender, and everything had to be sacrificed to cargo space. The cabin that was home to the boatmen and their families had to be a masterpiece of planning, and it was no place for the claustrophobic. E. Prothoroe, writing in 1897, described the living conditions: 'We were told by an old boatman that in his time one child would have slept across the top of the bed, another across the bottom, two would have slept under the bed, while yet two others would have sought Morpheus in a cupboard, leaving one to sleep on the table or elsewhere as best he could.' All this in a space 2·7 m (9 ft) by 2·1 m (7 ft)! Perhaps the colourful decorations were brought in to add a touch of gaiety to this uncomfortable life, or perhaps they were a defiant gesture aimed at passing train drivers.

For the boat children, the life could be hard and, in spite of educational legislation, many remained illiterate. Some recalled how they used to pick up the rudiments of reading from the large letters painted on the sides of railway waggons they passed along the route. But there were compensations. Winter, which brought ice, the boatman's worst enemy, gave the children the fun of the ice-breaker. Many still remember it with great pleasure. The ice-breaker was usually an iron boat with a high, wooden or metal frame running down the centre. As it was towed forwards, men in the boat held on to the rail and rocked backwards and forwards to break the ice under the keel. The main object of the children lucky enough to be allowed on board was to rock the boat with sufficient violence to slop the icy water over the side to soak the feet of their elders.

The narrow boat is a peculiarly British craft, but other craft were coming into use in Europe, where waterways were developed with great verve and enthusiasm. The British, who had scorned to look at continental models at the beginning of the canal age, showed an equal lack of interest in these new developments. The nineteenth century was almost over before any radically new ideas came to the British canals. Then, in 1885, an Act was passed through Parliament authorising the construction of the Manchester Ship Canal.

The early canal-builders would have been ecstatic at the sight of the equipment available to the new generation of canal engineers. There vere 58 steam-navvies, 97 steam-excavators and five dredgers; there vere 194 steam-cranes, 394 stationary steam-engines and pumps and 9 pile-drivers. Added to that were 173 locomotives with more than six housand waggons running on over 321 km (200 miles) of specially laid rack. Complementing the machines was a work force which, at its eak, reached a total of fifteen thousand. Work began in November .007 and was completed six years later. People came to marvel at the ew canal just as they had more than a century before at the Bridge-vater and, sadly, the old canal's greatest wonder was a victim of the ew. Barton aqueduct was demolished, but in its place the engineer, eader Williams, erected a swing aqueduct—a new wonder to replace he old. The swing aqueduct, as its name suggests, pivots on a central upport and the entire trough, complete with its water, can be moved hrough ninety degrees to make way for the tall vessels using the Ship Canal.

The Manchester Ship Canal turned out to be a last grand gesture o canal construction. Private capital was no longer available and, in ny case, construction costs and land costs were now too high to make uch an investment practicable. The government could have supplied noney, but they would have been backing waterways at the expense of he privately owned railways, or so the railway companies argued. Then he internal-combustion engine brought a new form of transport to the oads, and even the railways themselves were threatened. Canals con-inued their slow slide towards decay and closure. Some routes have lisappeared altogether leaving hardly a trace, while others have left a ew pathetic reminders of former glories: bridges that no longer span nything at all, a name here and there—Canal Street, Wharf Lane, the Navigation Inn.

At the end of the Second War War, the old canal companies were inally ended. As part of the government's nationalisation policy for ransport they were taken over, with a few exceptions, by the Docks and nland Waterways Executive of the British Transport Commission. One of the more telling comments on the state of canals at that time vas a notice put out by the Executive: 'CAUTION. The following offences re punishable under Acts of Parliament or Byelaws: Trespassing, Bathing, Damaging Fences, Throwing Refuse, Live or Dead Animals nto the Canal.' From being a busy commercial network the canals had legenerated into unofficial dumps for rubbish, live or otherwise.

The Executive spent money on improving the still commercially iable waterways, and took an important step as far as the future of canals was concerned, by starting to run pleasure-boats for hire. It was not a new idea. Pleasure-boats had run from the earliest days, and a century before a perspicacious gentleman, a Mr Robins, had written in his *History of Paddington*: 'The shares of the Grand Junction Canal Company are below par, though the traffic on this silent highway is still considerable; and the cheap trips into the country offered by its means during the summer months are beginning to be highly appreciated by the people, who are pent in close lanes and alleys; and I have no doubt that shareholders' dividends would not be diminished by a more liberal attention to their want.'

By 1963, when the British Waterways Board was formed to take over the running of the canals, the pleasure-boat business was well established and growing fast. It is still growing. The idea that canals can be enjoyed is now firmly entrenched. Local authorities are beginning to see canals as amenities rather than obstacles, and schemes such as the Cambrian Wharf development in the heart of Birmingham have demonstrated how great an improvement can be made to the environment when canals are treated with imagination. But, sadly, for every Cambrian Wharf there are still miles of semi-dereliction, where the only interest in the canal appears to be taken by football supporters and by John who announces to the world with aerosol spray that he loves Jane

Nevertheless, the future of the old narrow canals seems assured. The thousands of holiday craft provide a scene as busy as at any time since the days when canals were the latest thing in the world of transport The days of commercial traffic on the network, however, are virtually at an end. But that does not mean that there is no future for commercia traffic on the whole of the network. There is a lot being done and a lo more that could be done to use parts, at least, of our inland waterways

Waterways have always been best suited to moving bulk cargoes, and they are certainly better fitted to take such commodities than are many of our overcrowded roads. According to figures published by the Waterways Board in December 1973, water transport still remains the most economical way to move goods, if we ignore those that can be moved by pipeline. For the same cost, one ton of freight could be shifted less than 6·4 km (4 miles) by air, 93·3 km (58 miles) by road, 321·8 km (200 miles) by rail and 402 km (250 miles) by water—an impressive figure Yet the waterways are underused. In the north-east of England there is a busy trade on the Aire and Calder where coal is moved between colli- eries and power-stations in special 'trains' of boats, rather like the old tub-boats, and known by the curious name of 'Tom Puddings'. Thi ystem has been greatly improved by the introduction of push-pull tugs, which do precisely what their name suggests. Other waterways in use n the area include the Sheffield and South Yorkshire, although, at the ime of writing, this waterway is working at only a fraction of its posible efficiency due to lack of funds for essential modernisation. The hip-canals continue in use, though traffic has declined on the Gloucester and Sharpness.

After all the gloom it is pleasant to be able to end this brief historical urvey with a look at an exciting new development that promises well or the future of water transport. The use of containers that can be oaded off lorries and trains into specially designed container ships is vell-established. Now, however, a new process has been developed. The ontainers are loaded into specially designed barges which can then be ecured to a mother ship, taken across to Europe and there, with no xtra handling, the barges can continue their journey down the extenive and modern waterways of the continent. There are two main ystems in use: LASH (lighter aboard ship) and BACAT (barge aboard atamaran).

The first BACAT carrier was launched in September 1973, to do ervice on a route between north-east England and Europe. The ships ake 10 BACAT barges, each of 140 ton capacity, which are raised from he water by a shipboard elevator and secured on the deck, and three LASH barges, each of 370 ton capacity, which are left in the water, ecured between the twin hulls of the catamaran. The potential of such raft is enormous. Loads could, for example, be brought by motorway o special inland ports on the edges of cities and towns, so that there vould be no need for heavy container lorries to try and force their way hrough crowded city streets. There can hardly be a city dweller in Britain who would not welcome such a development.

BACAT and LASH are realities, but it still remains to be seen how ar their potential for easing traffic in our overcrowded island can be ealised.

Other, grander, schemes are raised from time to time, of which much he most ambitious was a plan put forward in 1942 by a Welsh civil ngineer, J. T. Pownell, for a 'Grand Contour Canal'. This envisaged a new broad waterway which would follow the 94·5 m (310 ft) contour ine, linking together major cities and ports, starting at Southampton and passing through Birmingham, Leicester, Leeds, Manchester and Newcastle. Will it ever be built? Will it ever be seriously considered? Without a special canal crystal ball, the question has to be left unanswered, but past experience suggests not. So, if asked to look into the future, my prognostication would be that the main canal network we have inherited from the eighteenth-century pioneers will continue to give delight to thousands of holiday-makers, while the commercial developments will be concentrated near the sea-ports, where they could again play an important role in the pattern of British transport.

5 CANALS FOR PLEASURE

There is a great deal of pleasure to be had from walking along canal tow-paths, and tens of thousands of anglers pursue their sport from the banks. But all writers should be allowed to exercise their prejudices occasionally, and now is the time to exercise mine: canals were built for boats and quite the best way to enjoy them is from a boat. For the majority of people this means hiring a boat for a canal holiday, and a lot of people are put off the idea by not knowing what to expect. They are not at all sure about coping with staircase locks and swing bridges and other minor problems, such as steering the boat or losing the odd child or two overboard. So before going on to describe the system that is there for the travelling, here are a few notes intended to help the beginner. Experienced canal travellers can safely move on to the next section.

Anyone considering a canal holiday needs certain basic information: he needs to know where to go and how to go. The next chapter gives a series of thumb-nail sketches of the canals which should help in deciding on what route to take, but it is impossible to select a route without some idea of how far you can travel in the time available for your holiday. A comfortable rate of travel on the canals is 4·8 km (3 miles) an hour, but that assumes an uninterrupted passage—and that is something you rarely find. There are not many canals where you will not meet a few locks in the course of a day's journey. Someone worked out a useful measure called the 'lock-mile', which is regarded with deep scorn by many enthusiasts who have long since forgotten their own early problems, but which is a very convenient way of working out how far you can get in any given period of time. To use lock-miles add on an extra 0·8 km (½ mile) for each lock, so that, for example, a 16 km (10 miles) stretch of canal with 4 locks would count as 12 lock-miles, or 4 hours cruising time at 4·8 km (3 miles) per hour. Using lock-miles, the Llangollen Canal from Hurleston Junction to Llangollen, which is 71·6 km (44½ miles) long with 21 locks is 55 lock-miles or about 18 hours' travelling time: in other words it is a comfortable 3 days' journey or a round trip of one week. It is important to remember when planning a trip, that hire firms almost invariably want boats back where they started.

The next choice facing the hirer is where to get a boat and what type of boat to get. Obviously the choice of base must depend on the chosen route: there's not much point in looking at boats in Oxford if you are thinking of a week on the Leeds and Liverpool. Even so there will generally be a wide range of alternatives on most canals—wide-ranging in terms of both quality of boat and cost of hiring, though with respect to the latter it is always as well to see exactly what you are getting for your money. Addresses are easy to find: hire firms advertise in the press, there are special holiday guides and hire firms can be found listed in the British Waterways Board guide-books. It is always as well to get a few brochures to see just what will best suit your needs.

Choosing a boat for canal cruising is largely a matter of individual preference, and what follows is simply one person's view, and that view can be expressed very simply: in my experience the best boats are steel narrow boats with tiller steering. In part, to be honest, the choice of a boat based on traditional lines, is sheer romanticism, but there are practical reasons as well. Canals tend to do a lot of winding about and they are crossed at frequent intervals by bridges which reduce the width of the channel. Boats cannot just be flicked round bends, and the great advantage of tiller steering is that the whole length of the boat is in sight in front of you and you have very precise control. The steel boat, too, is an advantage, for it tends to sit easily in the water and not get sent scuttling off course by cross winds. They are so simple to manage that even a child can steer them—my own daughter could handle a boat even when she could only manage to see over the cabin roof by standing on tiptoe.

Having chosen a canal and found a boat to travel in, what can you look for in a canal holiday? The type of scenery depends on where you choose to go, but all canal holidays have certain features in common: for a week, or however long you go, the pace of life is blissfully reduced. You travel at walking pace, and the modern world and the rush of traffic hardly seem to touch you in the closed, almost private, world of the canals. Mind you, unless you take a holiday on a hotel boat, there's work to be done. There are no officials to work locks for you: on the canals it's strictly do-it-yourself. It can be hard work, but there is a sense of achievement in working a boat efficiently through a flight of locks—though some claim that it is mere masochism. Like many activities, canal travel is pleasanter and you are less likely to have accidents if you know what you are doing. The rules for canal use are simple, and largely a matter of common sense. Ignoring the rules only makes you a nuisance to other craft and would probably land you in difficulty. So here are a few basic rules and some tips.

The first point for concern is safety, particularly when young children are on the boat. Canals are not usually very deep, little more than a metre (three or four feet), but locks are very deep. It is a sensible precaution to keep children in life-jackets, which most hire firms will supply. For everyone, adults and children, proper footwear is essential—avoid leather soled shoes or other shoes liable to slip. When you jump on board it is on board you want to be, not overboard.

Canals have a speed limit of 6·4 km (4 miles) an hour and most boats will not travel faster. Do not try and make them do so. Extra revving merely digs you lower into the water and extra speed, if you could get it, would damage the canal. In general stick to the middle of the channel where the water is deepest, except at bends when the deep water is on the outside. When passing other boats coming towards you, move to the right so as to pass port to port. Overtake round the starboard side of the boat in front. It's as well to get these rules firmly in your head as there are few things more irritating for canal users than to find a boat that insists on turning back in towards you instead of away from you.

One other important set of rules are the slowing down rules: slow down when going under bridges, slow down passing moored craft, and if you see working boats don't just slow down but get right out of the way—you're having fun, they're earning a living. One last point on this topic: boats don't come fitted with brakes, to stop you have to reverse the engine and it takes time.

Obstacles on the canal are mainly locks and bridges. Bridges are easily dealt with, provided you remember that the channel does not go under the middle of the arch: slow down and keep an eye on the gap between the edge of the boat and the towpath. If you keep near that edge you needn't worry about the other side. As well as fixed bridges, there are also movable bridges, although the term 'movable' sometimes seems a bad joke. Lifting bridges are easier to deal with, just hang on to the rope or chain suspended from the overhead balance beams on most bridges, and your own weight pulls the bridge up, though it's a good idea to keep hanging on, for it is not unknown for bridges to come down again of their own accord. Swing bridges, on the other hand, can be fiendish things: over the years the platform ends tend to drop and catch on the ground. Moving them then becomes really hard work. Fortunately they are comparatively rare.

Locks are the main worry for beginners, and many hirers will give a demonstration to novices. In fact, they are simple to manage. First of all, stop the boat some way from the lock to let whoever is going to work the paddles get out, taking a windlass with them. Stay well clear of the lock until the gates can be opened, otherwise the boat is buffeted by the strong current caused by the water passing into or out of the lock. For those working the lock the things to remember are: that the paddles at the lower end let water out and those at the top let water in, and, most importantly, that one set should never be opened until the other is closed, and a lock must never be left with any paddles open. It is a good idea, especially with light boats, for someone to hold the lines to stop it bumping around in the lock—but don't try and tie up a boat that is going down or you end up suspended from the ropes. One more point—keep the stern clear of the top gates when going downhill, for below the surface is a stone sill and you don't want to get caught on it.

Like all rules written out at length, these tend to look alarming, but they sound more complicated than in fact they are. Working a lock is simple common sense. Paddles go down quicker than they go up, but common sense indicates that it is better to let them down gently to avoid damage, than to let them just fall under their own weight. Common sense also suggests that to leave a windlass on a paddle is dangerous—if the paddle slips then the windlass is liable to fly off into the lock.

The rules governing mooring are common sense too. If there are mooring rings on the bank use them—they are there because the water is deep and you won't get stuck trying to get off. If there are no rings, you have to drive spikes into the ground, but don't let the mooring ropes cross the tow-path. If someone trips over and breaks a leg, it is you who gets sued and you pay the damages. Never moor where you are obstructing other boats, and never moor part way down a flight of locks.

What sort of things can go wrong? Far and away the most common mishap is running aground and getting stuck. The Waterways Board are understaffed and dredging is not always all it should be on all canals. So it happens to us all. If you stick, first try and reverse, gently, and usually you will come clear. If that doesn't work, ease the bows out from the bank by pushing away with a pole or boat hook and then push the stern out into deeper water and again reverse until you are clear. The main thing is, don't worry about it—everyone gets stuck. Other problems might arise, but it would be tedious to run through the lot and it might make a canal trip sound like a commando assault course, which it is not.

To reiterate: common sense avoids most problems and solves the rest. Never be afraid to ask questions of the hirer before you take a boat out: he would rather tell you what's what than have you damage his boat. A proprietor of one hire business tells of a party who arrived insisting that they needed no advice, and set off rather as if they were taking a Cunard liner out of Southampton. The helmsman gave his orders in a suitably captainly style and the crew cast off. Alas, they cast off by throwing the ropes from the boat and sailed away leaving their mooring ropes still fastened to the rings. The hirer, being a kindly soul, chased after them and saved them having to spend the night holding the boat into the bank with their hands. The moral is obvious: it's better to ask questions and risk being thought an idiot than not to ask them and prove that you are one.

6 CANAL PROFILES

The following profiles are character sketches, intended to give a general idea of what a particular canal is like and to emphasise just a few of the points of special interest. Because this is a book about canals and not about inland waterways in general, discussion of rivers is kept to a minimum and is only included where a particular stretch of river is used to join different parts of the canal system. The list is not complete, but I have tried to cover the canals which are likely to be travelled by pleasure-boats. After that I have listed some canals which, though not navigable at the time of writing (spring 1974), might possibly be restored in future years. The section concludes with a few places of special interest on the canals which can be visited on a day out.

Lancaster Canal

The route begins nowhere in particular and ends in a very similar place, for this canal has suffered badly over the years and much of the old route has been lost. Originally, the canal ran from Preston, where it met a railway connection; to Kendal at the edge of the Lake District. It still starts in Preston, if some distance from the original terminal, but sadly it no longer reaches Kendal. Some 24 km (15 miles) short, with the hills of Lakeland tantalisingly near, the canal comes to a miserable and abrupt end, running slap into a giant embankment, built to carry the A6070 over the M6 motorway. Tow-path walkers can pick up the route on the far side of the bank, but the boatman can only turn sadly back and return the way he came.

But one must not dwell too long on what has gone when so many delights remain. Leaving Preston, the route is at first pleasant if unspectacular, but as one moves north the scenery becomes steadily more varied and interesting. Where else could one get off a canal boat and have the choice of walking in the hills or swimming in the sea? The Lancaster Canal, running close to Morecambe Bay on the west and skirting the Pennine hills to the east, offers these choices.

The Lancaster, as one would expect from a canal engineered by John Rennie, has some of the finest examples of high quality masonry work to be found anywhere on the canals, and the Lune aqueduct at Lancaster is the outstanding masonry aqueduct in the country. It is not the highest, being only 18 m (60 ft) above the river, but in its severe classical styling and perfect proportions it is far and away the most handsome. Even if there were nothing else to commend the Lancaster, the Lune aqueduct alone would make the trip worth-while.

The main canal is lock-free throughout its length. But anyone who feels that a canal holiday without a lock is no holiday at all can make a detour near Galgate, where a short arm takes the canal down through six locks to Glasson basin and the Lune estuary. The docks at Glasson are still busy with yachts and sailing dinghies and it makes a pleasant overnight mooring.

The Lancaster is isolated, having no direct connection with other canals, so that there is a comparatively limited number of boats available. This is a disadvantage in some ways, but on the other hand it means that the Lancaster combines superb scenery with fine canal architecture and has the virtue of being one of our least crowded waterways.

Navigable length 67·5 km (42 miles); no locks. Glasson Arm 4·8 km (3 miles); 6 locks.

Leeds and Liverpool Canal

The Leeds and Liverpool presents a fascinating mixture. It was begun in the very early days of canal-building, its enabling Act was passed in 1770, and, inevitably, James Brindley was called in to advise, though the route had first been surveyed by John Longbottom. But, looking at the canal today, there are not many signs of Brindley's work, for although work was begun in 1770 it was not finally completed until 1816. Delays were partly caused by the difficulty of thrusting a very long route across the Pennines and partly by chronic cash shortages. In 1768 Brindley and Robert Whitworth produced a detailed estimate of the costs, which they calculated at £259,777. In the event they were proved a little optimistic, the final cost running to around £1,200,000—an almost Concorde-like escalation. So along the route we can read the history of canal engineering—in parts wandering and doubling back upon itself as it follows a level round the hills, in other parts striding boldly on high embankments or charging up the hillside in a great staircase of locks. And just as the engineering shows remarkable contrasts, so too the canal-side scenery is full of variety.

Starting at the Leeds end, the canal begins close to City Station at a junction with the Aire and Calder. It is an interesting place and presents the first of the contrasts. The older Navigation is still in use and steam-

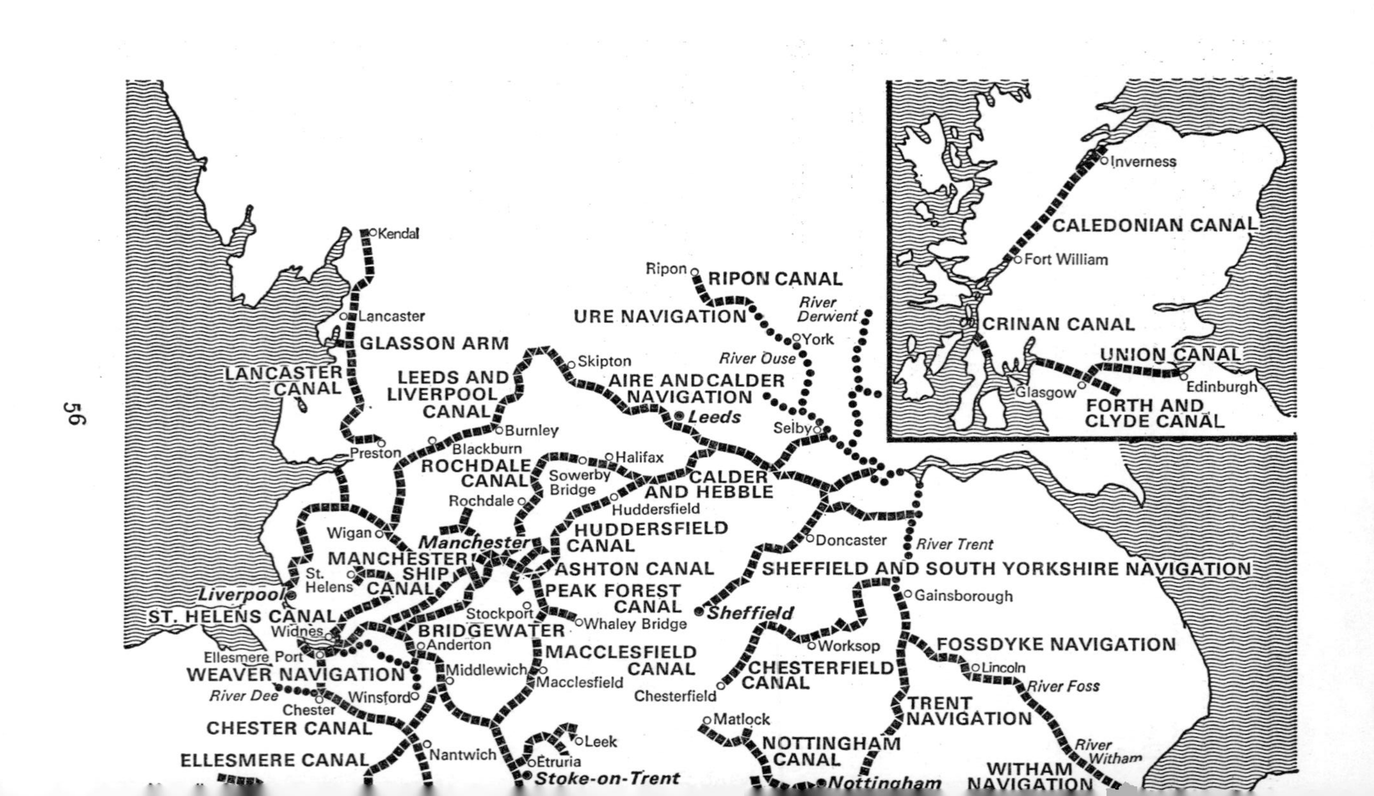

CALEDONIAN CANAL
Inverness
Fort William
CRINAN CANAL
UNION CANAL
Edinburgh
Glasgow
FORTH AND CLYDE CANAL
Kendal
Lancaster
GLASSON ARM
LANCASTER CANAL
Ripon
RIPON CANAL
River Derwent
URE NAVIGATION
York
River Ouse
Skipton
LEEDS AND LIVERPOOL CANAL
AIRE AND CALDER NAVIGATION
Leeds
Selby
Burnley
Blackburn
Preston
Halifax
ROCHDALE CANAL
Sowerby Bridge
CALDER AND HEBBLE
Rochdale
Huddersfield
HUDDERSFIELD CANAL
Wigan
Manchester
Doncaster
River Trent
MANCHESTER SHIP CANAL
St. Helens
ASHTON CANAL
SHEFFIELD AND SOUTH YORKSHIRE NAVIGATION
Liverpool
PEAK FOREST CANAL
Gainsborough
ST. HELENS CANAL
Stockport
Sheffield
Widnes
Whaley Bridge
BRIDGEWATER
Anderton
Worksop
FOSSDYKE NAVIGATION
Ellesmere Port
MACCLESFIELD CANAL
WEAVER NAVIGATION
Middlewich
Macclesfield
CHESTERFIELD CANAL
Lincoln
River Dee
Winsford
Chesterfield
River Foss
Chester
TRENT NAVIGATION
CHESTER CANAL
Matlock
Leek
NOTTINGHAM CANAL
ELLESMERE CANAL
Nantwich
Etruria
River Witham
Stoke-on-Trent
Nottingham
WITHAM NAVIGATION

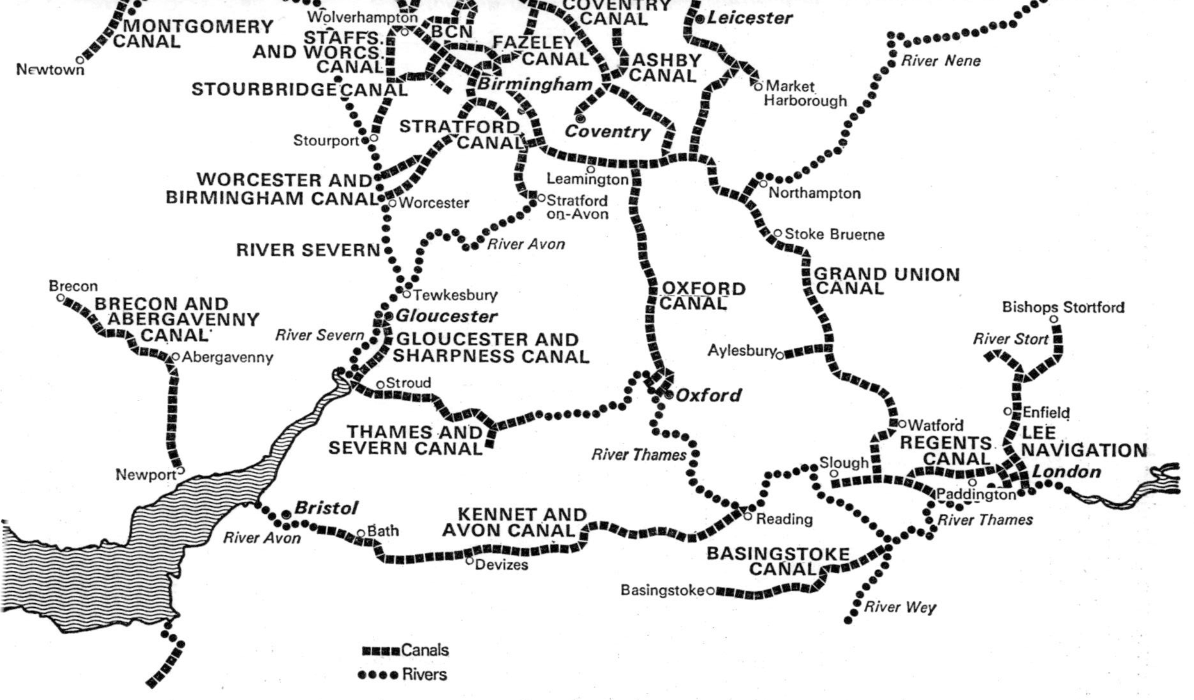

The Principal Canals of England, Wales and Scotland.

cranes chug along, loading barges at the busy wharf, while across the water the canal company warehouse, which once proudly served the 'modern' canal, looks out over an empty wharf. It is, however, a handsome building and an invitation to the city council to make a start at turning the canal in Leeds into a public amenity.

Once the canal has cleared the rather depressing first few kilometres through industrial estates, it takes a far from unpleasant meander along the Aire valley, passing a variety of interesting buildings, ranging from the smoke-blackened ruins of Kirstall Abbey to the Mackeson brewery. It is not long, however, before one meets the first of the swing bridges, which occur regularly along the route. For those interested in architecture, the canal passes the mills and houses of Saltaire, named after its founder Sir Titus Salt, who combined mill-ownership with philanthropy and laid out a model town for his mill-workers. But, returning to the canal, one is now approaching one of the engineering marvels of the canal—the Bingley Five, once romantically known as the Great Lock.

The canal passes above Bingley itself, and one negotiates a three-lock staircase before rounding a bend to find the Five looming up ahead, ready to take you 18 m (60 ft) up the hillside. To pass through the five wide, inter-connected locks is one of the great experiences of the canals. This marks the beginning of a 27 km (17 mile) stretch of lock-free travel, but then Bingley certainly satisfies one's urges for locking for a good while. At the top of the locks is the stone lock-cottage and if you look carefully the details of large painted letters are just visible. They arrived there because the cottage was built of stones from an old company warehouse that was demolished in Liverpool, and which had the company name written on it. In re-using the stones the order was changed, producing today's faded jigsaw.

Westward from Bingley, the canal enters the most beautiful section of its long line, and indeed one of the most beautiful of any canal in Britain. The scenery is Pennine, the scenery of the dales, and in parts the canal is joined both by the Yorkshire Dales National Park and the famous walking route, the Pennine Way. Towns near the canal are few, and the only place of any size that the canal passes is the lovely old market town of Skipton. A short branch passes alongside the walls of Skipton Castle, though it is not easily navigated and town and castle are best seen on foot. Moving on from Skipton, the canal becomes more and more remote from civilisation and the countryside itself becomes wilder. Past Gargrave and Bank Newton locks, the canal is forced into a serpentine route as it squirms and twists around hill and hummock against a background of distant peaks and moorland. This section ends with a plunge, some 1500 m (1640 yds) long, into the darkness of Foulridge tunnel. Tunnels such as this are either exciting and fascinating or boring black holes, depending on the individual's point of view. I like them and most children love them, if only for the ear-splitting racket they can make by shouting in them; but some hate them—each to his own.

Beyond Foulridge the canal again changes character. Now it passes through a series of towns whose names epitomise Lancashire cotton—Nelson, Burnley, Blackburn, Wigan, Leigh. Whether one likes this stretch depends on how one views such places, but the canal enthusiast has much to enjoy. There is, for example, the great embankment that sweeps high above the rooftops of Burnley, itself a depressingly nondescript town since modernisation has clothed it in anonymous plastic. Canal travellers get the best of it, however, passing between the towering mills and warehouses that line the bank—and those on the look out for the unusual might like to know that the canal also passes a tripe works. Many of these old towns are often dismissed as a bad joke. Wigan, for example, is everybody's idea of a joke town, but a closer look reveals an amazingly elaborate, almost Baroque, Victorian architecture. And you certainly get plenty of time to see Wigan—there are twenty locks! There is, too, a fine wharf area with a jetty that must surely be the famous Wigan Pier.

Beyond Wigan, towns and open country alternate until the canal reaches Liverpool, first passing Aintree where it lends its name to the Canal Turn on the Grand National course. The end, when it comes, is an anti-climax. Beyond Aintree, the route is little used, swing bridges are locked to prevent vandalism and a special key has to be obtained by anyone who actually wants to go on to where the canal ends in a filled-in section some four hundred metres from the original terminus.

Most pleasure-boating on the canal is confined to the central Pennine section, but the western end is also used by boats moving on to the Bridgewater Canal and the eastern end has its connections via the Aire and Calder to the Trent.

Total length 220·5 km (137 miles); 85 locks.

Bridgewater Canal

This is something of an oddity in being privately owned by the Manchester Ship Canal Company. The majority of boats one meets on the canal are those using it as part of a through route to the Leeds and

Liverpool at Leigh or to the Trent and Mersey at Preston Brook. But, in its own right, it deserves a special place in the affection of all canal enthusiasts as the first true canal in Britain.

The beginning of the Bridgewater Canal is at Worsley Delph, no more than a metre or two from the M62. Here the canal emerges from the old mine-workings, stained by ore to the colour of tomato soup—a curious sight. What one cannot see today is the extensive system of underground channels that stretch for many kilometres from the insignificant opening in the hillside. But just round the corner is the handsome canal basin, a picture post-card setting, with its fine old black-and-white buildings. It is here that the Leigh branch of the Leeds and Liverpool comes in.

From Worsley the canal runs on towards Manchester, crossing the Ship Canal by the Barton swing aqueduct. This is normally left open for Ship Canal traffic, but is swung back hydraulically on roller bearings to take boats on the old canal. The line to the centre of Manchester now swings away to the east, but the main line continues westward towards Preston Brook. On the way it passes over the river Bollin by a high bank and aqueduct, and it was here, in August 1971, that the canal broke its banks and the whole came tumbling down in a serious breach. The breach served to underline the anomalous position of the Bridgewater, and also to demonstrate just what a vital role it still played in the system as a whole.

At Preston Brook, the broad Bridgewater turns to meet the narrow Trent and Mersey. It is a delightful spot—in spite of a new motorway bridge—with attractive cottages and a large brick warehouse which someone, quite unaccountably, has painted to simulate stone. The route goes on to Runcorn, where once it locked down to the Mersey, but now simply ends.

The Bridgewater Canal is remarkable as a piece of engineering, broad and lock-free, but, to be honest, not very attractive. Where once it went to meet Manchester, now Manchester has come to meet it and the canal never quite seems able to shake off the suburban sprawl of the city and its surrounding towns. However, anyone travelling its broad waterway cannot help wondering what water transport in Britain would be like today if subsequent canals had been constructed to the same generous proportions. Would there still be a thriving commercial life? They were not built to this scale, so we shall never know.

Length 44·2 km ($27\frac{1}{2}$ miles).

Trent and Mersey Canal

The Trent and Mersey, or the Grand Trunk as it was known in Brindley's time, is a long route and one very popular with pleasure-boaters. It is also a canal historian's delight, full of associations with the past, the sort of waterway that can be explored over and over again and still reveal fresh secrets. Like the Leeds and Liverpool, it is a canal of contrasts, if not quite such dramatic contrasts. At its heart lie the Potteries, the driving force that brought the canal into being, and throughout its length reminders of the hectic days of the industrial revolution alternate with stretches of tranquil countryside.

The canal's northern beginning is certainly unspectacular in one sense. Near Preston Brook is a stop-lock with a fall of 15 cm (6 in) and a toll-house: these are the signs that one is leaving the Bridgewater and entering the Trent and Mersey. But if there is no 'grand entrance', there are two tunnels which although not very long, tell us a lot about the difficulties facing the early engineers. They follow a winding course, partly brick lined and partly bare rock; they are low and narrow with no tow-path, an interesting contrast to the new Harecastle further down the route. Once out of the tunnels, the canal follows a lovely hillside route, shaded by trees, with occasional breaks giving wide views of the valley and the river Weaver below. After a few miles of this one reaches one of the nineteenth century's best-known additions to the canal—the Anderton lift. What a marvellous thing it is. At first sight it looks like the work of some canal Heath Robinson or a mad meccanoist, but it still works and moves boats between the canal and the Weaver 15·7 m (50 ft) below. It was built in 1875, and originally the two tubs in which the boats float to be carried up or down counterbalanced each other, but in 1908 the lift was modernised and each tub, or caisson, was given its own set of counterweights, which can be seen hanging like so many giant clock pendulums around the framework, and the motive power has been changed from steam to electricity. Anyone wanting to try a trip on the lift has to pay a fee, which at the time of writing was £3 for the round trip.

Beyond Anderton is a rather different kind of modernisation: the straight course indicates immediately that the old line has been altered. In fact we are among the salt mines, and the Marston New Cut was built because engineers thought there was a danger of subsidence from the old workings. How right they were: only a few weeks after it was opened the ground gave way and the old canal vanished. This section was once a broad canal, though all that is left as a reminder is one lock at the foot of the flight leading to Middlewich. Next to it is a large Victorian industrial complex, not especially notable in itself, but having its own odd little pub, *The Big Lock*, built into it.

Beyond Middlewich the canal enters its least attractive section, and really it is difficult to find anything to commend as modern industrial developments give way to a wilderness of mining flashes and spoil heaps. Thankfully it does not last long and one is soon back in open country. Because this was such a busy route, it has been greatly modified to speed the flow of traffic, the most obvious improvement being the doubling of the locks to save waiting time. But because doubled locks need extra water a culvert was built between the two, so that when water was lowered in one lock half of it could pass into the next.

This is still an industrial area, but the industries are old and passing time has mellowed their buildings. Old mining communities with their rows of cottages and wharfs and warehouses now seem just part of an attractive canal-side scene, and indeed they are so right visually in their setting that it is hard to remember that they have any industrial connection at all. There is hardly a harsh note in the landscape until one comes upon the startling sight of Thurlwood steel lock. The old lock was collapsing from mining subsidence, so this new experimental lock was built: a giant steel box closed at either end by guillotine gates Whatever other distinctions it may have, it is certainly the ugliest lock in Britain.

From Thurlwood there is an irritating straggle of locks, just far enough apart to make walking a nuisance but close enough to make it hardly seem worth-while getting in and out of the boat: not too bad on a fine day, but a miserable chore on a wet one. Approaching Kidsgrove one meets a canal flyover as the Macclesfield Canal passes overhead on an aqueduct before coming in to join the line a little further on. Here is a flight of locks, the Red Bull flight, and it is interesting to see how lock and junction call a whole complex of buildings into being. Half way up the flight is a maintenance yard, at the top there is a tollhouse to cover the junction and as this is an enforced stop for boats, shops and the inevitable pub turn inviting faces towards the canal.

Beyond Kidsgrove are the Harecastle tunnels: on the left the low entrance to Brindley's original, on the right the much larger opening to Telford's tunnel. Originally, it was planned that the two tunnels should both be used, one to take northbound traffic the other to take southbound, but with the collapse of the old tunnel Harecastle is again a bottleneck. There are regulations governing the use of the tunnel: al users have to get clearance from the tunnel-keeper, as there is no room to pass inside the tunnel, and at weekends northbound traffic is allowed through in the mornings only and southbound in the afternoons. As regulations can change, always check first if you are planning a trip to include Harecastle.

It is a long journey and coming out of the southern end, you are in a new world, the world of the Potteries. Once the skyline was dominated by the bottle kilns, and though these have almost all disappeared, the industry still dominates the canal-side. Works which once used the canal as their main line of communication often stand with their walls sheer to the water, and mooring rings and loading bays are reminders of earlier days.

Most famous of all was the Wedgwood works at Etruria, but little of that now remains. Wedgwood's home, Etruria Hall, still stands, desolate among the coal waggons, peering across at Shelton Steelworks through which the canal takes a spectacular passage. By bridge 118 there is a small, round building with a conical roof, Wedgwood's modelling shop. Almost all the rest has gone. But not quite. Close to the bridge is a row of terraced cottages that once held the families of Wedgwood's workers. Late in the nineteenth century a Trent and Mersey boatman gave up the water for the land, acquired two of the cottages and converted them into a pub, *The Bridge Inn*. It is still there, its interior hardly changed, china pump handles and all. In Stoke the still navigable Caldon arm turns off but the main line continues on, reaching the new Wedgwood works at Barlaston, a factory set in lovely parkland. After that the Potteries are left behind.

The canal now returns to something closer to its original form: locks are the single, narrow type; bridges come in all sorts of shapes and sizes representing, to a large extent, the tastes and whims of the individual builders. The route passes areas such as Chartley Moss and Cannock Chase that scarcely show the passage of centuries. Other canals start to come in from the west, first at Great Heywood where another Brindley canal, the Staffs and Worcester, appears from under a lovely, low, pointed arch bridge; then the Coventry appears at Fradley Junction. This is one of the most popular and most photographed of canal sites: set in open countryside is a small group of buildings, including the maintenance yard and the *Swan Inn*, all of which owe their existence to the canal by which they stand.

For the remainder of its course, the canal follows the Trent valley, even using the river itself for part of the way. This is a less busy section

than some parts of the canal, and if pottery dominates the forme
section now, in its swing back to the north-west, it is beer that sets th
boatmen's noses sniffing, for the route passes the breweries of Burton-
on-Trent. Otherwise the passage is peaceful, apart from the occasiona
unwelcome attentions of the busy A38 road which keeps the cana
company for some of the way.

The Trent and Mersey ends in its very own inland port of Shardlov
which contains just about the most beautiful set of old warehouses
wharfs and pubs one could find. It is almost as if a major port had bee
taken, shrunk and popped down in the middle of the country. It is, o
was, a marvellous spot, but already the vandals are at work and mellov
brick is being bulldozed to make way for developers' anonymity. Beyon
the tiny town, the canal ends in the waters of the Trent.

Total length 151·3 km (94 miles); 78 locks.

Trent Navigation

The Trent is an essential link between the Trent and Mersey and th
canals of the north-east. It has a reputation for being a dull river, an
even its best friends would have to admit that some reaches lack charm
Certainly on leaving the Trent and Mersey one gets off to a bad start
the view is dominated by the M1 and a power-station and indeed ther
is little enough to please the eye until Nottingham is safely astern. The
the river makes up for its beginnings by entering a lovely rural reach
with wooded hillsides standing high above the eastern bank. A featur
of the route is the number of ferry inns, so very different from the cana
pubs. They have a vaguely 1920s air about them, reminding on
irresistibly of gay divorcees and one still expects to find refugees from
Ben Travers farce scuttling around among the rooms. For those wh
value the peaceful life. weekdays are the time to travel, for at weekend
the Trent comes to life: the river is crowded with boats and otherwis
peaceful spots, such as Gunisthorpe, are swamped by trippers, fun-fair
and the furious activity of water-skiers.

Newark marks a major change in the character of the river. Fror
here onwards commercial traffic claims pride of place. But the tri
through the town itself is splendid and more than ample compensatio
for the drabness of Nottingham, culminating as it does at Newark castle
its oriel windows standing out over the water. But now pleasure-boat
must move with care. A few kilometres further on is Cromwell, and th
start of the tidal reaches and very sparse moorings. The best stoppin
places are to be found in the many turnings off into other waterway

1 Where the canal age began: the Bridgewater Canal emerging from Worsley Delph.

2 Brindley's Oxford Canal winds through the landscape at Napton.

3 The simple but satisfying style of canal architecture: lock cottage at Somerton, Oxford Canal.

4, 5 *Opposite* The Staffs and Worcester Canal: *above* Near Kinver; *below* The octagonal tollhouse at Bratch.

6, 7 Georgian Stourport: *above* The main basin; *below* Canal-side warehouse.

The Trent and Mersey Canal and the Potteries; *opposite*. Bottle kiln at Longport; *top* The *Bridge Inn*, Etruria; *below* The Etruscan Flint Mill.

Overleaf Working narrow boats at Stoke Bruerne.

B. & M.C.C.C.L^TD
BIRMINGHAM
Nº
7

PICTOR
PICTOR

12, 13, 14 Canal bridges: *opposite above* A simple brick design on the Chesterfield Canal; *below* Mass production without ugliness, a Horseley Ironworks bridge on the Oxford Canal; *above* A flourishing bridge at Somerton, Oxford Canal.

15, 16 Warehouses: *top* Pickfords at Worksop, Chesterfield Canal; *below* Mellow brick at Shardlow, Trent and Mersey Canal.

17 *Below* Cruising the Oxford Canal at King's Sutton.

18 Cheddleton Flint Mills, with machinery by Brindley, on the Caldon branch of the Trent and Mersey.

19 Arched loading bay in a towering warehouse, Rode Heath, Trent and Mersey Canal

THISTLE

20, 21 *Opposite* Recent additions to old canals: *top* The M6 crossing the Staffs and Worcester; *below* Barton swing aqueduct opening for traffic on the Bridgewater Canal.

22 *Below* The Anderton lift that takes boats from the Weaver Navigation up to the Trent and Mersey.

23 The Rochdale Canal near Hebden Bridge.

24, 25 *Opposite* The Leeds and Liverpool Canal: *above* Passing through the Pennines at Bank Newton; *below* The five-lock staircase at Bingley.

26 Unusual double-arched bridge at East Marton, Leeds and Liverpool.

27 Mills and warehouses lining the route of the Leeds and Liverpool through Burnley.

28 Britain's longest canal tunnel: Standedge tunnel on the Huddersfield Canal.

29, 30, 31 Aqueducts: *below* Brynich aqueduct on the Brecon and Abergavenny Canal; *opposite above* Dundas aqueduct on the Kennet and Avon; *below* Marple aqueduct on the Peak Forest Canal.

32 Rennie's masterpiece: The Lune aqueduct on the Lancaster Cana

35 Autumn on the Kennet and Avon near Pewsey.

33, 34 *Opposite: top* A flotilla of geese on the Kennet and Avon; *below* Boys fishing on the Peak Forest Canal.

36 A major problem for restorers: the derelict Caen Hill flight near Devizes on the Kennet and Avon.

37 The Kennet and Avon at Bath.

38 Supplying water to the Kennet and Avon: The water-wheel that powers the pumps at Claverton.

39 The cylinders and valves of Crofton's steam-engines.

41, 42 *Opposite* The great aqueduct of Pont Cysyllte on the Llangollen Canal.

40 The Brecon and Abergavenny Canal at Mamhilad.

43 Cruising on the high bank near Pont Cysyllte.

44 A derelict canal due for restoration: a lock on the Montgomery.

GENERAL CARRIERS
TO
CHESTER, LIVERPOOL,
MANCHESTER,
NORTH, AND SOUTH, STAFFORDS
AND
NORTH WALES.
NDFORD BRIDGE
CHESTER
DGE CANAL CRUISERS

Opposite top Swabbing the decks at Ellesmere, Llangollen Canal.

Opposite below Lock-cottage at Tyrley on the Shropshire Union.

The Shropshire Union Canal skirting the city walls at Chester.

48 *Above* High bridge over the Woodseaves cutting, Shropshire Union Canal.

49 *Opposite top* Deep cutting near Church Eaton, Shropshire Union.

50 *Opposite below* A bridge guard plate showing the grooves cut by countless tow ropes.

51 Langley Maltings on the Titford Canal, BCN.

THE LONG

54 *Above* Canal in the Black Country: Delph flight on the Dudley Canal.

52 *Opposite top* A bright new canalside development at Cambrian Wharf, Birmingham.

53 *Opposite below* A private world in the centre of Birmingham, Gas Street basin.

55 *Above* The recently restored Park Head locks on the Dudley Canal

56 *Opposite top* Evening on the BCN

57 *Opposite below* Cruising the BCN at Spon Lane

NORTHUMBERLAND
OLD WHARF TARDEBIGGE

60 *Above* Building over the canal, Brindley House, Birmingham.

58 *Opposite top* Starting up Britain's longest flight at Tardebigge, Worcester and Birmingham Canal.

59 *Opposite below* The junction house at Kings Norton.

61 *Opposite* Contrasts on the Macclesfield Canal; *above* The elegant
62 Ramsdell Hall; *below* Fairytale cotton mill at Bollington.

63 The Waterways Museum beside the locks at Stoke Bruerne, Grand Union Canal.

64 Ornamental bridge over the Grand Union at Cassiobury Park, Watford.

65 A peaceful scene where navvies once rioted, the *Navigation Inn* at Barrow-on-Soar.

66 Canal pubs: The *Globe Inn* at Linslade on the Grand Union.

67 The horse gets the first drink at Solbury locks.

70 A popular pastime: watching boats cope with the Foxton staircase on the Grand Union.

68, 69 *Opposite* The Grand Union: *above* The daunting sight of Hatton locks; *below* Cruising past Marsworth reservoirs.

71 Winter on the Grand Union in Cassiobury Park.

72, 73 *Opposite* The canal in London: *above* Day-trippers on the Regent's Canal passing London Zoo; *below* Little Venice.

WATER NYMPH

GLAMIS CASTLE

4 Entering Laggan lock on the Caledonian Canal.

OCEAN MIST

75, 77 The Caledonian Canal: *above* The deep Laggan cut; *opposite top* Passing Ben Nevis.

76 *Opposite below* The sea-locks and basin at Crinan.

78 Working boats passing through Solbury lock, Grand Union Canal.

79 Pleasure-craft passing dredging tips at Cowley Peachy, Grånd Union Canal.

80 The impressive array of nineteenth-century warehouses at Gloucester Docks.

81 Modern commercial traffic on the canals: BACAT barges at Doncaster.

82 Coal barges and oil tanker at Ferrybridge.

83 A contrast to Britain's narrow canals: a new, broad waterway in West Germany.

85 The canal in its industrial revolution setting: the Rochdale at Todmorden.

86, 87 Working boats: *above* A pair of powered narrow boats on the Oxford Canal; *below* A rare sight—the horsedrawn boat *Hyades* on the Grand Union.

88 Number Ones: Joe and Rosie Skinner on their boat *Friendship*; *inset Friendship* on an inn sign.

89, 90 Commercial traffic today: *above* A convoy of Tom Puddings; *below* The Narrow Boat Company's fleet on the Ashby Canal.

91 Boating for pleasure. Llangynidr locks on the Brecon and Abergavenny.

92 Pause for a pint on the Oxford Canal.

93, 94 *Right* Lifting bridge at Wrenbury on the Llangollen Canal; *below* Cruising on the Leicester section of the Grand Union.

96 *Opposite* Canals in town and country: *above* The Leeds and Liverpool at Skipton; *below* The Shropshire Union at Audlem.

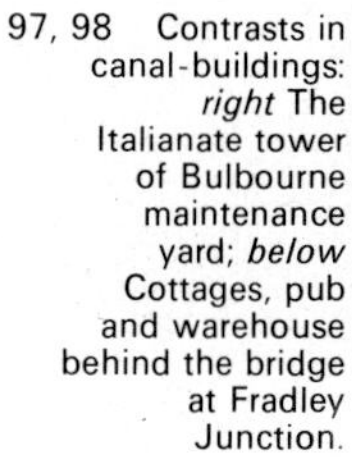

97, 98 Contrasts in canal-buildings: *right* The Italianate tower of Bulbourne maintenance yard; *below* Cottages, pub and warehouse behind the bridge at Fradley Junction.

99, 100 *Above* A split bridge on the Stratford Canal; *below* Swing bridge and bridge cottage on the Gloucester and Sharpness Canal.

101 Curious pedestrian tunnel under the Grand Union at Cosgrove.

102, 103, 104, 105 Changing designs in aqueducts: *above* Brindley's aqueduct carrying the Staffs and Worcester over the river Sow; *below* The first iron trough aqueduct at Longdon-on-Tern. *Opposite top* Edstone aqueduct on the Stratford Canal; *bottom* The Grand Union crossing London's North Circular Road.

ICL

106, 107 Motorways and Canals: *above* The M6 in Birmingham; *below* Westway and the Grand Union in London.

08, 109 Decay seen in an abandoned bridge on the Lancaster Canal *(above)* and in a lock full of rubbish on the Rochdale.

110 Restoration: lock rebuilding on the Caldon arm of the Trent and Mersey.

he first being the old Fossdyke that leads away to Lincoln. The traveller ontinuing past this turn has the dubious reward of having three ower-stations in view at the same time.

Gainsborough offers a busy waterfront and good moorings, but as ne goes on the river traffic becomes heavier and the scenery entirely isappears, the flat Lincolnshire plain being hidden behind high banks. Only ferries and junctions provide a break and a chance to see anything esides other boats. West Stockwith marks the entrance to the Chester eld Canal and further on Keadby lock gives access to the Sheffield and outh Yorkshire. Here sea-going freighters load and unload on the iver which continues, steadily widening, until it reaches the Humber stuary at Trent Falls.

Small boats can use the tidal Trent above Gainsborough, but great are should be exercised. Always advise lock-keepers when you expect o arrive, otherwise you run the risk of being stranded on a mud bank or ft to drift in the centre of the channel for the night, and neither fate is o be recommended.

ength—from Derwent Mouth to Trent Falls: 149·6 km (93 miles); 2 locks (operated by lock-keepers).

heffield and South Yorkshire

'he pleasure-boat traffic on this route is very largely confined to those aving the Trent and making their way across to the Aire and Calder. 'he canal is navigable, but comes to a dead-end, if that is not too harsh way to describe the rather splendid Sheffield Basin.

This canal is one of the few where someone else does most of the work r you, for the many swing bridges are manned. Whether you enjoy the rst part of the journey depends on whether you like the Lincolnshire ountryside and trains, for the land is flat, the canal is straight and the uch-used railway line follows it all the way. The route is busy with oats carrying fuel for the Thorpe Marsh and Doncaster power-stations. lans to improve the waterway and increase its efficiency have been ound for some years but, at the time of writing, decisions have not yet een reached. So one is still treated to the sight of the most modern ssels being manhandled through locks, just as if we were in the ghteenth century—a ludicrous misuse of an amenity.

After 24 km (15 miles) the New Junction Canal comes in at an acute gle, to run dead straight for 8 km (5 miles) before joining the Aire d Calder. Those continuing on the main line will find a few stretches here the canal passes through open country and rather more through

towns and the landscape of modern industry. Towns visited includ-
Doncaster, of which the less said the better, and Rotherham with it
often dramatic views of steelworks. The end of the canal at Sheffield ha
a dull approach, far from typical of this pugnaciously interesting city
but the terminal itself must certainly be ranked among the two or thre
most important examples we have of large-scale canal developments.
Length 69 km (43 miles); 28 locks.

Chesterfield Canal

Another Trent connection but, as the eastern end is now derelict,
dead end. It is intriguing to compare the busy South Yorkshire with th
quiet Chesterfield, and whereas the former ends in a fine basin, th
latter begins with one. West Stockwith hides behind the high lock gate
that lead up from the Trent, but once reached all is delight and charr
and one is back to the smaller scale of the narrow canals. For those wit
a taste for curiosities, a few hundred metres away, where the Idle joir
the Trent, is a flax mill, built in 1748, and once powered by an ol
Newcomen engine, although only the engine-house and water tank nov
remain.

The route is pleasant, rural and peaceful, but quite the best par
comes with the passage through Osberton Park, a fine landscaped are
created when Osberton Hall was built in 1806. Early canal promote
used to extol the delights of a canal as an addition to the stately hom
scene, and the Chesterfield provides ample justification for thei
enthusiasm.

The route ends, abruptly, just beyond the old Pickford warehouse i
Worksop.
Navigable length 41·8 km (26 miles); 15 locks.

Macclesfield Canal

This is one of the Trent and Mersey's most important connections, an
one that will undoubtedly be attracting more and more traffic over th
next few years. The Macclesfield only just made it into the canal age–
creeping in at the tail end of the period, and almost suffering th
indignity of being replanned as a railway. It made it, however, a fa
for which all waterways enthusiasts should be suitably grateful. Th
route begins at Hardings Wood Junction and once it has doubled bac
over the Trent and Mersey it heads north. The special character of th
canal soon asserts itself, with the view to the east dominated by the hil
of Derbyshire, the first of which is Mow Cop, crowned by its curiou

eighteenth-century folly, a mock ruined castle. These hills also proved a convenient source of supply of the building-stone which can be seen in the many beautiful bridges that span the route.

The canal runs past the sloping lawns of Ramsdell Hall and on through pleasant, open country until it reaches Congleton. There, just before the town wharf is reached, is the first of the Macclesfield's famous 'snake' bridges. Beyond the wharf, the canal crosses the road on a short cast-iron aqueduct, and if experienced canal travellers think it looks a little familiar, then they are right, because the same casting was used for the aqueducts on the Shropshire Union main line.

Beyond Congleton the canal passes, via a number of high embankments, through beautiful country to the one set of locks, the flight of twelve at Bosley. This splendid flight lifts the canal 30·5 m (100 feet) up the hillside, giving superb views over the hills and distant moorland. Macclesfield itself is now only some 8 km (5 miles) off, and those who don't know the town could well be pleasantly surprised, for it combines its present function as a market town with remnants of old industry, including the distinctive homes of the silk-weavers. The textile industry comes into its own, however, at Bollington where the mills line the banks and include one genuine oddity. Just beyond the town wharf is a nineteenth-century mill, all turrets and parapets, looking as if it was designed by Disney for a production of Snow White and the Seven Little Cotton Operatives. From here to Marple, the canal completes its journey with a pleasant and quiet progress through woods and fields.

At Marple, the end of the line, there is ample evidence that the local people enjoy the canal: houses along the route seem never to hide behind hedges or walls, but open out to the canal and many have boats moored at the end of their gardens, whether shiny new cruiser or humble rubber dinghy. Past the houses, the canal meets the Peak Forest.

Length 44·2 km (27½ miles); 12 locks.

Peak Forest and Ashton Canals

It is only in the spring of 1974 that these two routes were reopened for navigation, and very welcome they are too. From its junction with the Macclesfield, the Peak Forest swings away north to the Ashton Canal and Manchester, where it rejoins the Bridgewater. But before considering this route, it is worth looking at the section to the south, where the canal completes its journey to Whaley Bridge. No one should miss this part of the canal if they can possibly spare the time to visit it, and as it is only 10·4 km (6½ miles), the return journey can be fitted comfortably into a day.

The route to Whaley Bridge begins in truly spectacular fashion with a passage along the hill-top high above the Goyt valley. The route is lock-free, but full of interest. Anyone concerned with the history of canals can have a fascinating time tracing the many tramway connections, and there are a great many as one would expect from a canal engineered by the tramway expert, Benjamin Outram. One can often find the sidings and wharfs where the two met, for example, at bridge 31 at Furness Vale. But the most interesting example is at Whaley bridge itself, where the route ends in a unique canal–railway interchange, a covered terminus with the waterway running in at one end and the rails of the Cromford and High Peak Railway running out at the other.

Back at Marple and continuing the journey northwards, the canal plunges on down through the town by a flight of sixteen narrow locks. They might seem hard work, but there is plenty to see along the way, which takes one's mind off the exercise. At the upper end of the flight the short pounds between the locks have been widened out into large ponds, making a pleasant outlook for some lucky householders, but really there in order to ensure enough water for the canal. There is a lovely little horse-tunnel under the main road, and half way down is a warehouse with a covered loading bay. This was an important point on the canal, and there is also a small tollhouse covering the road access to the wharf. Further down, the flight leaves the town behind, the last lock is negotiated and suddenly one is high in the air, crossing the valley on the magnificent Marple aqueduct. Incidentally, the large circular holes in the spandrils, the supporting arches, are not there for decoration but to lighten the load of the structure.

Beyond the aqueduct the canal makes the most of the lovely countryside, with open fields and heavily wooded slopes providing the scenery before it slips into the great urban sprawl from Manchester. At Ashton the canal of that name is reached near the junction with the Huddersfield Canal. So often coming into cities and large towns by canal one gets the worst aspects—how very pleasant then, to be able to record that here at least one fares rather better. Some of the local industries along the route have been persuaded that a canal can give pleasure, that if properly looked after it is an ideal place for people to sit and fish, walk about or just do nothing, so they have opened out to the canal instead of skulking behind barbed wire or high walls. They have made the canal an amenity to be enjoyed by their own workers and by everyone else. Let us hope others copy.

Coming into the centre of Manchester, the Ashton meets the Rochdale Canal, and the last kilometres are Rochdale water. Other sections of the Rochdale have been improved, but at the expense of making them unnavigable—a kind of one step forwards three steps back improvement. Finally, at Castleford Junction, we are back again at the Bridgewater Canal.

One final word about the upper Peak Forest—the swing bridges are especially difficult to move, so take a strong friend.

Lengths Peak Forest 23·3 km ($14\frac{1}{2}$ miles), 16 locks; Ashton 14·4 km (9 miles), 18 locks.

Shropshire Union Canal

As its name suggests the Shropshire Union is not one canal but an amalgam made up of the Liverpool and Birmingham, the Chester and the Ellesmere canals. The main line runs from Ellesmere Port on the Mersey to Autherley on the outskirts of Wolverhampton, and as the different sections were constructed by different companies at different times, it provides some interesting contrasts. But, for most people, it is simply thought of as one canal and is, rightly, one of the most popular. However, starting at the northern end does not lead one straight in to the popular sections.

Ellesmere Port was once the pride of the canal system. Here Telford built a great port, with ranges of covered warehouses and extensive docks. In theory they were scheduled for preservation, in practice fire broke out and they were razed to the ground. There was a sad irony about the event for myself: I had made a special journey north to take a detailed look at the site and arrived just as the bulldozers were moving in to clear the rubble from the fire. I missed my inspection by a day. However, to return to the canal, the route south to Chester is known as the Wirral line and was constructed as part of the Ellesmere Canal Company's programme of expansion. It was built as a narrow canal and the port that was founded at its northern end has become an important industrial centre. But as industry has developed, the canal has declined, and the little-used route is often clogged with rubbish of every conceivable kind.

The traffic today mostly goes no further north than Chester, where the canal circles the high rocks and walls of the old city like a moat, before reaching an extensive area of old docks and warehouses with cobbled streets leading back to the city centre. We are now on to the old Chester Canal, built as a broad canal with locks 4·5 m (14 ft 9 in) wide. Its main trade was in Nantwich salt and, of course, Cheshire cheese, and one sees far more of the agricultural side of its trade than one does of any industrial concerns. The route closely follows the line of the river Gowy, and the length of the river is spotted with old water-mills. There are no great excitements on the Chester Canal, no spectacular features, but it is a wonderfully relaxing waterway, hardly touched by the modern world. For those with eyes to see there are no end of visual pleasures: the tiny circular lock-lobbies, where a lock-keeper could sit cosy and snug when trade was not too heavy; lovely old mills such as Christleton, built in a series of changing angles to follow the curve of the canal; the splendid stables at Bunbury locks and the adjoining warehouse, which has the company's initials spelt out in the brick-work. Passing the reservoirs at Hurleston, which keep the canal supplied with water, one also passes the entrance to the much famed Llangollen or Welsh Canal, and reaches Nantwich, where one leaves the Chester Canal behind and enters the Liverpool and Birmingham Junction.

At once it is clear that this belongs to a different generation of canal-building, very different from the leisurely wanderings of the old Chester line. Here are all the hallmarks of the 'modern' canal: a very straight overall line, locks grouped into convenient flights, iron aqueducts and, most significantly, alternation between high embankments and deep cuttings. It is the use of the cut and fill technique that gives the Shropshire Union its own very distinctive personality. Once the deep cuts must have been bare, ugly scars, but over the years the water draining down the sides has helped the spread of a luxuriant growth of plants. After rain, the green walls steam, branches and tendrils of creepers loop down overhead, so that the passing boatman feels he is in a tropical jungle, a sort of Sanders of the cut.

South of Nantwich basin, the first of the small aqueducts crosses the main road and one is almost immediately on a long straight section to the village of Audlem and the flight of fifteen locks that lift the canal 28 m (93 ft) up the hill. At the foot of Audlem flight is a much favoured stopping-place, with a typical group of canal-side buildings. There is a lock-cottage, which itself is very typical of Telford's architectural style, a pair of small warehouses and a pub to provide refreshment for those who have just worked down the flight, or to give strength to those about to work up it. It is a pleasant, open flight and at the top there is a brief respite before the five Adderley locks are reached, after which there is a clear run through to the attractive town of Market Drayton. That this was once an important canal site is obvious from the large warehouses around the town wharf.

Beyond Market Drayton one meets the Shropshire Union at its very best. You come at once on to a high bank that carries the canal over a minor road and the river Tern, then the land rises ahead and you plunge into a deep cutting through richly coloured sandstone to the bottom of the short Tyrley flight. Many claim this to be the most attractive flight of locks in the country, and it is hard to argue. Closed in by trees, it is all contrasts, the red rock and the green leaves set against the crisp black and white of balance beams and paddle gear. Hardly clear of the locks, the canal plunges into the deep Woodseaves cutting, crossed by a tall high-level bridge. While admiring the surroundings, think for a moment about the scene when it was being built, with row upon row of barrows being hauled and shoved up the steep slopes as the navvies dug ever further down into the cutting. For this great gash in the earth was made by men armed with no more elaborate tools than picks and spades.

The alternation of bank and cut continues throughout the length of the canal, so there is no point in describing the same scene over and over again. There are, however, a few special points of interest to look out for. At Norbury there is a junction where a branch arm, now filled in, led away to Newport: opposite is the maintenance yard where all the different jobs of repair and replacement could be carried out. When it was new, power was supplied by a steam-engine, but now only its smoke stack remains, though there is still a forge for metal-work. The bank beyond the yard is the biggest on the canal, Shelmore Bank, which took five troublesome years to complete. Beyond that again is the rock cutting and tunnel at Cowley—the tunnel is unlined, so that you can still see the scars of pick and bore in the rock face. One aqueduct deserves a special mention, Stretton, for this carries Telford's canal over the Holyhead road, also engineered by Telford. He was clearly not unaware of the distinction, for he gave this aqueduct a slightly more elaborate treatment than the others on the route. Elaboration is even more grandly evident where the canal passes by Chillington Hall. The avenue leading to this very stately home is carried over the canal by a suitably stately bridge. Finally, a stop-lock, designed partly to halt boats so that they could pay their fees at the adjoining tollhouse and partly to stop the Shropshire Union taking precious water from the

Staffs and Worcester, announces the presence of Autherley Junction and the end of the line.
Length 107 km (66½ miles); 42 locks.

Llangollen Canal
Variously known as the Welsh Canal, the Llangollen Canal and the Ellesmere Canal, it is, in fact, part of the Shropshire Union. It is far and away the most popular with pleasure-boaters and, consequently, the most crowded. In the summer months, in particular, it is often overcrowded as boats queue to go through the locks, but out of season it remains as delightful as ever.

Inevitably, thoughts about this canal are dominated by the last quarter of the route, the approach to Llangollen. It is rather ironical that one of the most popular stretches of canal in the country should have been built not for its value as a navigation but to supply other sections with water. However, we will start by looking at some of the smaller, more intimate pleasures which are so often overshadowed by the grand and dramatic.

The first point to make about this route is that it is almost entirely rural: for kilometre after kilometre there are only farm-houses, surrounded by their fields and barns, and the occasional small warehouse where the farmer's produce can be stored for transport on the canal. Waterfowl and cattle are more common on the banks than people. The mood is pastoral, and picturesquely pastoral at that. Even the white painted lift bridges, so reminiscent of Holland and Van Gogh, seem to have been designed with the scenery as much as utility in mind. Lock-cottages, usually the work of local builders using vernacular styles and none the worse for that, are sometimes given a little extra grace, as at the three-lock staircase at Grindley Brook. Here the little cottage has a bow-front and verandah, so that it looks for all the world like a miniature refugee from Regency Brighton or Bath. The only town of any size is Ellesmere, which once lent its name to the canal, and to reach it the canal threads its way between lovely wood-encompassed lakes. At Ellesmere is the maintenance yard, a somewhat curious building in an odd kind of mock-Tudor. But if you look up to the roof there is a charming weather vane in the shape of a narrow boat. The town itself is reached down a short arm.

Past Ellesmere, the Montgomery Canal turns off to the south, and the hills of Wales loom ever nearer and the grand finale approaches. The first of the wonders is the Chirk aqueduct, a fine masonry structure, but now rather overshadowed by the taller and more grandiose railway viaduct at its side. Once across, the canal takes a smart turn and disappears into Chirk tunnel to re-emerge in the deep Chirk cutting. A short run, and the towering lime kilns of Fron Cysyllte are among the few reminders that this canal once served busy industries, and already the great aqueduct of Pont Cysyllte can be seen striding across the Dee valley. Nothing quite compares with the thrill of crossing Pont Cysyllte by boat. The trough is narrow and although on one side there is the comforting protection of guard rail and towpath, on the other there is only a low iron rim, actually below the level of the gunwales, between you and the valley 36·5 m (120 feet) below. After that anything might seem an anti-climax, but not here. The canal turns to run high above the valley to end on the hillside above Llangollen. The wharf marks the end of navigation, but a walk along the tow-path brings one to the Horseshoe Falls, not falls at all really, but a weir built so that water could be taken from the Dee to fill the canal.

Length 71·6 km (44½ miles); 21 locks.

Staffordshire and Worcester Canal

From the grand designs of Telford and Jessop we are back in the world of James Brindley. In fact, no better demonstration of the differences in canal engineering can be found than at Autherley Junction, where this canal meets the Shropshire Union. From the wide, deep cuts of the latter, one turns into a little rock cutting, which was such a problem to the earlier engineers that they could only make it wide enough for one boat to travel at a time and had to provide passing places, rather like those on some country lanes. The canal was built to join the Trent and Mersey to the river Severn, and we shall begin at Great Heywood Junction at the Staffordshire end.

The first part of the route is a canal oddity—Tixall wide. Here we are on the edge of the parkland of Tixall Hall, the massive gate house of which can be seen from the canal, standing now in complete isolation. There is a theory—unproved—that the canal was widened at this point so that the aristocratic owners of the Hall could imagine they had an ornamental lake at the end of the estate instead of a commercial waterway. The canal follows the route of the river Sow, crossing it once by a low aqueduct, and as the river wanders so the canal wanders to keep it company, under rows of low-arched brick bridges. This part of the canal is not left in peace, however, for it is soon joined by the M6. But even motorways find uses for canals, if not very dignified ones. Where the road crosses the canal, grilles have been left in the bridge so that storm water can drain on to the heads of unfortunate boatmen. Happily, the motorway is a brief visitor.

Penkridge is a good stopping place on the canal, and possesses another canal oddity. The road bridge has been built so close to the bottom gates of Penkridge lock that special alcoves have been built into the brickwork to allow the gates to be opened. The canal wanders on again, managing to keep its countrified appearance even as it skirts the edges of Wolverhampton. And once that is behind the canal comes into its loveliest reaches, starting with the famous Bratch locks.

The first three locks of the Bratch appear, at first sight, to be a staircase, but they are not: each is separated by a metre or so of water, and the curious must surely wonder why. The answer lies in the inexperience of James Brindley. This was his first narrow canal, and it seems that faced with the steep hillside the idea of running the three locks together simply did not occur to him. But he left us with this lovely flight, topped by its bridge and little octagonal tollhouse. The remainder of the route is marked by heavily wooded hills and sharp sandstone outcrops. An awkward, difficult terrain for the canal which twists and writhes to find a way through, sometimes running right to the base of the high cliffs.

The end of it all is at Stourport, Britain's first canal town. Two centuries ago, before the canal was built, only a lonely pub marked this spot where the little Stour flows into the Severn. Then Brindley, irritated by the refusal of the citizens of neighbouring Bewdley to see the advantages of his beloved canal, came here and chose it as the spot where canal and river should meet. So the present town grew, brought into existence by the needs of the canal and its busy trade. Here are the wharfs and warehouses, inns and stables, the homes of the new residents who came for the trade or to organise the port. Even today the area surrounding the canal is pure Georgian, with the handsome formality and sense of proportion that one associates with the period, and which we find in the commercial buildings as much as in the homes. The citizens of Bewdley must often have regretted the day they unwisely called Brindley's canal a 'stinking ditch'.

One last small feature of the Staffs and Worcester is worth looking out for. All canals have overspill-weirs at locks, to allow water to pass down the canal rather than flow over the top of the gates, but here they were built as circular brick weirs, like giant plug-holes, and are found on no other canal.

Length 74 km (46 miles); 43 locks.

Severn

The Severn is another river that forms a connecting link in the canal system, and is often cruised as part of a canal holiday trip. As this is a canal book, we shall just look quickly at those parts which might be used as connections.

Turning into the river at Stourport and heading south it is pleasant and peaceful, although after the narrow canal it seems exceptionally wide. The first turning back towards the canal system is near Grimley, where the Droitwich Canal goes away to the east. This is now derelict, but it may possibly be reopened. Continuing on down the steadily widening river one reaches the city of Worcester, dominated still by the great square tower of the cathedral. Trade has only recently declined on the river, and the wharfs by Diglis basin at the south of the city are newly abandoned. Here the Worcester and Birmingham takes its turn to lead back towards the Midlands. Those who continue downstream will find the river scenery progressively less interesting as it broadens yet further into its flat plain. The rewards for continuing include the opportunity of turning into the delightful, and only recently reopened, Avon Navigation to link eventually with the Stratford Canal, or going on as far as Gloucester and the Gloucester and Sharpness Ship Canal.

Worcester and Birmingham Canal

This is one way of returning from the Severn to the busy Midlands, but it is a way for the hardy. If your idea of holiday fun is working through locks, then this is for you: if not, keep away. The whole journey to Birmingham is only 48·3 km (30 miles), but in that distance there are 58 locks, and 30 of these are grouped together at Tardebigge, in the country's longest flight.

For those undeterred by the prospect of Tardebigge, the canal has a lot to recommend it. At first it provides a pleasant, rural route and in its later stages it gives access to the very centre of Birmingham while managing to remain surprisingly aloof from the city itself.

Once clear of the canal's beginning at Worcester, an attractive city that does not show its best face to the canal, a country mood is established. Nothing dramatic in the way of scenery, but all very peaceful and seldom crowded with boats. Locks form frequent interruptions to progress and at Dunhampstead the canal disappears into a short tunnel. Although there is no tow-path, the tunnel was not legged: the boatmen hauled themselves along by the handrails still set into the tunnel wall. Beyond the tunnel, although the canal is still rural, one gets a foretaste of industry as the canal passes the now abandoned ICI works. Will a later generation descend on the site with demands for preservation? Very probably—today's eyesore so often turns out to be tomorrow's romantic ruin.

By the time one reaches Hanbury Park, the locks are starting to arrive with alarming frequency, so here are a few points of interest to divert the mind from the work ahead. Look, for example, at Stoke Wharf. No doubt it was once regarded as an unwelcome modern development, but now few places could seem more romantically attractive. Tardebigge flight itself is built on a curve, so one is not too daunted by the sight of the whole flight at the start of the long climb. One good place to pause is lock 33, where there is an ingenious and unique bridge. It is cantilevered, attached only at one end so that, unloaded, the other end tends to rise from the ground, leaving a gap for a tow-rope to pass. The flight is difficult to get in view, but to see it at its most impressive, get up on the dam of the reservoir at the top of the flight. Water conservation and supply is always a major headache for canals, and here it is met by the reservoir from which water was originally pumped by steam-engine. The engine has gone, but the engine-house remains.

Once through Tardebigge top lock you can relax, for that is the last of the locks on the canal, and you are back to attractive open country. The only interruptions now come from tunnels, of which the longest by far is the 2·4 km (1½ mile) Kings Norton tunnel. Beyond that it is possible to turn off into the Stratford Canal. Continuing on into Birmingham is an odd experience, for much of the route is through deep, overgrown cuttings, or through parkland at Edgbaston, so that before you are quite aware of it, your boat is in the heart of the city at Worcester Bar.

The route ends in a triple junction, meeting the Birmingham Canal and the Birmingham and Fazeley. Once the canal ended in its own basin, Worcester basin, now known, less poetically, as Gas Street basin. What an amazing place this is, hidden away in the very heart of a great city, full of colourful painted narrow boats, and surrounded by old warehouses. It is a private, almost secret place, left behind by the busy work of development, intimate and human among the office towers.

Length 48·3 km (30 miles); 58 locks.

Gloucester and Sharpness Ship Canal

To complete a description of the Severn connections, it is worth mentioning this, the first of Britain's ship-canals. It was built to by-pass the ıwkward shoals and bends of the river, but is seldom approached by :anal boats as it now only connects the tidal reaches of the Severn and he disused Stroudwater Canal. It passes through flat, uninteresting :ountry, probably of more interest to bird-watchers than scenery-vatchers, for the Slimbridge Wildfowl Trust is very near the route. The nain interests for canal enthusiasts are the two termini and the swing ›ridges that are moved to let shipping through. Each bridge comes :omplete with a bridge-keeper's cottage, built in grand style like niniature mansions, if such things can exist, with impressive pillared ›orticoes.

The canal starts at Gloucester docks, once a busy and important nland port, notable for its grand array of nineteenth-century ware-ıouses, some of which are beginning to show signs of decay. Architec-urally, the most interesting is the 'Pillar Warehouse', which is carried ›ut over the tow-path on stout pillars that give it its name. Gloucester lid not forget the spiritual welfare of the boatmen, and there is still a mall seamen's church, tucked away behind the tall, glowering com-nercial buildings. Sharpness, at the southern end, is no less impressive vith its vast lock joining canal to river, and a frontage lined with ware-ıouses. The town itself, with its very solidly respectable nineteenth-entury villas, grew up with the canal.

ength 27·3 km (17 miles); 1 lock.

tratford-on-Avon Canal

'he Stratford Canal has a very real distinction in the modern history of anals, for it was the first to be restored and reopened specifically to ıeet the needs of pleasure-boating. The effort involved many different rganisations and individuals. The National Trust put in cash and uaranteed to maintain the southern end of the route, and a new eneration of navvies appeared. Whereas the old navvies had been riven to canal work mainly by poverty, the new came for the love of anals. Some of the volunteers, however, were more voluntary than thers: a large part of the work was done by prisoners and Army units. 'he canal was officially reopened in 1964, and has since proved very opular. No doubt the name has helped: somehow Stratford-on-Avon ›unds more likely for holidays than, say, Macclesfield or Leeds and iverpool.

The canal begins with something of a rarity, a guillotine lock, which what its name suggests: gates being raised and lowered instead of eing swung in the conventional manner. The first few miles are a

meander through Birmingham suburbs, but, like the Worcester an
Birmingham, the canal manages to keep itself to itself. Only when i
emerges from behind the protection of overgrown and wooded bank
does the canal give any glimpse of the city. Once clear of the suburbs
the canal moves into open countryside, where all is peace and tran
quillity for some 16 km (10 miles). It is as well to make the most of th
peace, for after a straggle of locks Lapworth looms ahead and th
prospect of hard work is clearly visible. The main Lapworth locks ar
roughly divided into two flights, nineteen locks in all. The canal is quit
heavy on locks, but they are in pleasant surroundings and the Stratfor
locks are associated with two unique features. The first is the quit
common iron split-bridge, built so as to allow the tow-rope to pas
through the narrow gap in the centre. The second is the distinctive
barrel-vaulted cottage. Legend has it that these cottages acquired thei
odd, arched-shape because the Company ran short of money and hande
the building job to the navvies, who, being used to building tunnels
built tunnel-shaped cottages. An entertaining tale, but quite untrue.

At Lapworth a short cut leads off to link up with the Grand Union
but the main line continues on its way to Stratford. There are no mor
long flights of locks on the route, but there is a steady descent. This i
irritatingly slow, because the lock culverts appear to have been mad
too small for the job so that the lock chambers take an age to fill. Bu
for those who ask no more than to be away from the crowded, bus
world and to spend days of tranquillity among open fields and woods
then the waiting is worth-while. There are also some features of interest
notably the iron aqueducts, the longest of which, the Edstone, carrie
the canal over road and railway. It is a graceless construction in itself
although it gives the boatman a pleasant bird's eye view of the sur
rounding countryside. The route passes a number of pleasant Warwick
shire villages and pleasant Warwickshire pubs, such as the *Navigation* a
Wootton Wawen, before almost losing itself in a sudden plunge betwee
looming buildings that mark the outskirts of Stratford. At first there i
little enough sign of the town's bardolatry, but suddenly the cana
emerges into its main basin by the river, right in the middle of a publi
park with the Memorial Theatre only metres away.
Length 45 km (28 miles); 55 locks.

BCN

Initials known to all canal enthusiasts: BCN stands for Birminghan
Canal Navigations, not one canal but a network, a maze of waterways

The BCN is a world of its own, divorced from the main life of the city it helped to prosperity. How many Brummies know that their city has more miles of canal than Venice? Not that one is likely ever to find gondolas in Birmingham, nor indeed can the canals offer sights of equal architectural glories. Yet there are thousands who find the BCN the most fascinating of all British waterways, and who will tell you that a lifetime is hardly long enough to explore and know it all thoroughly. So, in a few paragraphs such as this, the best one can hope to do is to give an impression of the main parts of the system. In the end though, you have to see it for yourself. You love it or you hate it: you are fascinated by its sturdy, hard character or you can see nothing but dirty backwaters threading through waste land and industrial slums. It is only fair to put in a word of warning: some of the less used side-arms contain an astonishing variety of rubbish. On a trip down the Wednesbury Oak loop I once collected a submerged and still unidentified object, which could only be removed from the propeller after half-an-hour's assiduous work with an oxy-acetylene burner.

The main line of the Birmingham Canal leads from the Staffs and Worcester at Aldersley Junction down to the centre of the city, where it branches off into the Worcester and Birmingham and the Birmingham and Fazeley. This main line, to complicate matters further, is not one line but two: the original, a typically wandering Brindley canal, and the new route an equally typical piece of nineteenth-century straight cutting by Telford. The route now followed is the Telford line, from which the older canal parts company as a series of loops. The BCN was built to serve industry and fed on coal, and industry dominates from the very start as the canal swoops down through the twenty-one locks of the Wolverhampton flight. This is no place to look for the picturesque, but on the main line you will find the quintessence of nineteenth-century canal engineering: the wide straight canal in deep cutting, the tunnel at Coseley, its double tow-path such a contrast to older tunnels, the handsome iron aqueduct that carries the Engine branch—an unromantic name if ever there was one—and the even more handsome iron bridge that carries the road over the deep cutting at Galton. The twentieth century, too, has added a new dimension to the canal scene as the motorway strides over and even through the canal on giant concrete pillars. The route ends at Farmers' Bridge junction, where the city has for once acknowledged the presence of the canals in an imaginative new development, which deliberately sets out to retain the atmosphere of the old by using cranes, cobblestones and canal boats. Even the tiny old tollhouse has been kept and adds to the atmosphere. Impossible to believe, coming here by water, that one is in the centre of the city, yet New Street station is only metres away.

If one now continues down the Birmingham and Fazeley, one is at once in a very different world. Here the old confronts the new in direct opposition. Descending the Farmers' Bridge flight the canal is overlooked by a mixture of buildings that crowd in on it. Some are begrimed and decaying Victorian, others are the towers of the new Birmingham which even, at Brindley House, overwhelm the canal by actually being built right over its course. Yet through it all, the canal keeps an identity. There are still the elliptical arches of worn brick bridges, the firm lines and smart black and white of lock balance beams, the contours of worn stone. The canal eventually leads out of Birmingham to meet the Coventry Canal at Fazeley Junction, passing through a flat, surprisingly empty landscape. But before it is quite clear of the city it passes straight through the centre of the Gravelly Hill motorway intersection, the notorious 'Spaghetti Junction'. One other place deserves special mention. When so many commercial concerns turn their backs to the canal, it is especially pleasant to come upon the Cincinnati Works, which turn a bright face to the water. Lawns and paths make it enjoyable for both the works' staff and passing boatmen.

Returning to the city and the BCN, pride of place among the remaining canals must lie with the Dudley. This joins the short Stourbridge, chiefly noted for the finely preserved glass cone that stands by the water, to the Birmingham main line. It begins among strange scenes and ends with stranger ones. Coming down the Delph flight the view is almost alpine, though the hills owe more to man than to nature and, whether you like or dislike it, you cannot deny its power. But the real wonder is Dudley tunnel, only recently reopened to traffic and the pride of the BCN. Like the old Harecastle tunnel, the Dudley is an underground labyrinth of side branches, and opens out into vast caverns. In Victorian times it enjoyed a certain vogue when concerts were held in the tunnel, though they can hardly have been popular with the musically sensitive. Dudley, if not the longest tunnel in the country, is undeniably the most fascinating.

There is hardly space to do more than mention other routes. The Wyrley and Essington, for example, though partly filled in, now follows an oddly rural route around Birmingham; the Tame Valley, which sounds pleasantly rural turns out to be less so, alternating between heavily industrialised areas and suburbia; the Titford is little used but has magnificent examples of old industrial buildings, particularly the nineteenth-century Langley maltings. The list sometimes appears infinitely extendable. Perhaps the BCN is for those who have already come to love canals rather than for those making a first acquaintance, but for anyone who has once felt the fascination it is unique.

Coventry Canal

This connects the Trent and Mersey with the Oxford Canal by a route that skirts around the eastern side of Birmingham. There are two inescapable aspects to the Coventry. The first is that its twists and turns must have had their origin in the planning of its original engineer, James Brindley—though the Coventry Company are unique in being the only concern who actually dared sack the great man. The second is that it was built to serve the coal trade. Coaling wharfs, terraces of miners' cottages and mining spoil heaps are to be found all along the route: there are many urban sections, some showing an attractive face, others a drab, and none is drabber than unlovely Nuneaton.

The Coventry Canal may never make the holiday-makers' top twenty but it is by no means devoid of interest. Hartshill maintenance yard, for example, is a particularly fine example of canal architecture. Originally, of course, the main connection of the canal was with Coventry itself and it still reaches the city's centre. This section is not much used, which is a pity for it is a particularly pleasant way of visiting the city. Another interesting set of canal buildings is at Hawkesbury junction. The area is somewhat overshadowed by a wasteland of shrub-covered spoil heaps and the chimneys and cooling towers of a power-station. But, if you can close your eyes to that lot, you will find a really attractive site. Here are inn and cottages, lock-cottage and tollhouse, and the rather gaunt nineteenth-century engine-house that once housed a pumping-engine. The entrance to the Oxford Canal is spanned by a really fine, low arched iron bridge, cast at the Britannia Works in Derby.

Length 52·3 km (32½ miles); 13 locks.

Ashby Canal

A turning off the Coventry Canal, the Ashby is unusual in being lock-free throughout its length, so that anyone looking for a thoroughly lazy trip could hardly do better than this. It is unusual, too, that in running as it does near Nuneaton and one of the less attractive parts of the Coventry, it should itself have such a very different character. It is, incidentally, a good route for all kinds of historians: it is crossed by

Watling Street, it passes by Bosworth Field where Richard III made his unsuccessful bargain offer of a kingdom for a horse, and, coming nearer the present time, a railway museum has been established at Shackerstone on a disused line. There is something pleasantly ironic about leaving a still-used canal to visit a disused railway.

The Ashby Canal is remote from the modern world, passing through quiet countryside with little evidence of its old life as a busy coal canal. Only a few coaling wharfs remain, such as that at Stoke Golding, now converted for use as a hire base. Little used, peaceful and always attractive, the Ashby Canal has a good deal to commend it.

Length 35·4 km (22 miles).

Oxford Canal

The Oxford Canal suffers from a severe case of schizophrenia: from Oxford to Napton it is a perfect example of an eighteenth-century contour canal, from Napton to Hawkesbury the style is all nineteenth century. It was the opening of the Grand Junction that caused the split. The importance of the northern section grew as rapidly as that of the southern end declined. Inevitably, the northern end was improved, the lines straightened and duplicate locks built. When this major surgery was completed, the northern section looked more like the Grand Junction than its own southern half.

From Hawkesbury Junction southwards, the straight line predominates with high embankments giving views of open countryside and, less attractively, the M6. Branches lead off at regular intervals spanned by elegant iron bridges made at the Horseley Ironworks. In fact, they indicate where the old route went, swooping off on one of its many curves. These are interesting to follow, although no longer navigable. At Stretton, for example, there is the old Brindley aqueduct with its low brick arches. There is a fascinating story about this. When it was first built, a local dignitary, Sir Francis Shipworth, could see it from his home, so, deciding to make the best of it, he planted the surrounding area with trees and painted the whole structure. Another interesting branch to follow is at Newbold, where the old tunnel now stands disused beside the church. Newbold's new tunnel is a typically high and wide nineteenth-century construction, and at its southern end is a very pleasant and popular mooring with an old warehouse and two pubs. There's a curiosity here, too, but a more modern one: not surprisingly one of the pubs is called *The Boat*, though the pub sign suggests that the present owners must be rather ashamed of the humble canal because their sign shows a large yacht beating through a heavy sea.

Beyond Newbold the canal approaches Rugby, where in term time the descendants of Tom Brown can regularly be seen puffing along the tow-path on cross-country runs. At Hillmorton there is a lovely group of old buildings with engineer's house and maintenance yard beside the double locks, though the scene has now been marred by a new and ugly bridge. The canal now runs straight down to Braunston where it meets the Grand Union. For 8 km (5 miles) one travels westward on the new route, then at Napton Junction the old Oxford swings away again to the south. Improvements are now at an end and ahead lies what is justifiably regarded as one of England's loveliest routes.

Turning on to the southern Oxford, one comes to a canal hardly touched by the modern world, in fact hardly changed at all since its building two centuries ago. Immediately one loses the straight lines of the northern part as the canal curves around the windmill-topped hill at Napton and begins to climb through the straggle of narrow locks to its summit level. From here the canal proceeds to wind around every hillock and bump in the countryside, including the famous, or to working boatmen infamous, Wormleighton bend, where the canal tries its best to turn itself into a moat by almost completely encircling the hill. The long descent begins at the Claydon flight, and below Banbury the route so closely follows the line of the Cherwell that it, too, seems to be more of a river than a canal, and at one section the two do briefly combine. Where the river and canal meet, the difference in level is taken up by a special weir lock. Shipton Weir Lock has a fall of only 76 cm (2½ ft), instead of the more customary 1·5 m–1·8 m (5 ft–6 ft): if it were built to the normal width it would not pass enough water down the canal and would thus act as a dam. The problem is solved by a rather curious wide lock, the extra width making up for the loss of depth. The end of the canal is its junction with the Thames. This is most easily made by the short Duke's Cut, some 4·8 km (3 miles) north of Oxford, but the canal can be followed into the city itself.

The attractions of the southern Oxford are difficult to describe, they are made up of so many small things. The pleasure of mellow red-brick buildings has something to do with it. The cottages beside the narrow locks are not architect-designed but the work of local builders, using the vernacular style of the time. The result is that no two are quite the same, each has its own special character. The same unconsciously elegant style is found in purely functional buildings, such as the stables and main-

tenance building at Claydon Top Lock. The charm has also to do wit
the way in which one can so easily lose a sense of time on a canal such a
this, which wanders through green fields and under old hump-backe
bridges and simple lift bridges. The busy world almost fails to touch i
though at Banbury the eye is assaulted by the bus station that back
right up to the lock, and at Upper Heyford the ear receives an eve
worse shock as the canal passes the end of the runway of the busy Amer
can airbase.
Length 124 km (77 miles); 42 locks.

Grand Union Canal

The Grand Union is, as its name suggests, an amalgam, made up of
number of canals, of which the most important is Jessop's Gran
Junction. Overall, the Grand Union is a long route, stretching all th
way from London Docks to the outskirts of Birmingham, with branche
to Leicester, Northampton, Aylesbury and Slough.

Before setting off on the journey north, we shall look at the canal i
London, starting with the section still known by its original name—th
Regent's Canal. The middle part of the canal is well known, the end
rather less so. The canal begins its journey where it almost sneaks out c
the busy traffic of Limehouse Reach on the Thames via a now largel
disused basin. It then scuttles away among the factories and houses o
the East End. There is a brief burst of greenery at Victoria Park, the
it's back to the buildings. At Islington the canal disappears undergroun
for 800 m (½ mile), but it re-emerges from the tunnel to a section c
great liveliness. From Kentish Town onwards the route is busy wit
traffic, as trip-boats bustle past each other, full of sightseers. The mai
attraction is Regent's Park, where, in a pleasantly leafy cut, one find
oneself under the inspection of all kinds of exotic animals from th
neighbouring zoo. Here, too, is the best-known canal bridge, Maccles
field Road bridge, more commonly known as Blow-up Bridge, from a
accident in October 1874 when the barge *Tilbury*, with five tons c
gunpowder on board, blew up directly beneath it. The bridge wa
reassembled, but in the rebuilding the iron Doric columns were re
versed, for the groove cut by towropes now face away from the canal
Originally it was planned that the canal would be a centre piece to th
park, but the authorities changed their minds and it was banished to it
present route round the edge. Just beyond the park is Maida tunnel an
beyond that Little Venice, the perfect demonstration of how valuabl

an amenity the canal can be. All the same it's an inappropriate name—Little Amsterdam would be a much better analogy.

The Paddington Arm of the Grand Union leads away from Little Venice, overshadowed by Westway, passing the eerily baroque tombs of Kensal Green Cemetery, where a meeting with Count Dracula and his friends would not seem out of place, on to Wormwood Scrubs, exactly as attractive as the name suggests, and through the suburbs of north-west London. One great pleasure is to travel the route in the rush hour, when one can smugly cross a short aqueduct over the solidly jammed lines of traffic on the North Circular Road. The arm returns to the main line at Bulls Bridge Junction.

The main line proper begins by the Thames at Brentford, where the canal enjoys a busy commercial life, which might prove busier still in the future. No doubt all canals have their devotees, but I have never enjoyed the first part of the Grand Union as it leaves London. Once the suburbs are cleared, you arrive at gravel pits; gravel pits over and it's back to the suburbs. There are incidental pleasures in occasional mills and cottages, but for myself it has an overall dullness that is not quite shaken off until the canal enters Cassiobury Park, just north of Watford. Here at last is something to enjoy wholeheartedly, parkland laid out in the seventeenth century for the Earl of Essex, parkland with which the canal has come to terms and to which it has made its own contributions, especially one lovely ornamental bridge.

In spite of a steady succession of towns, the Chiltern hills ensure a welcome variety in the scenery as the canal climbs steadily towards the long, heavily wooded cutting at Tring, which ends at the Bulbourne maintenance yard. It looks a little odd with its Italianate tower, but here the traditional canal crafts are carried on, including the manufacture of the wooden lock-gates and balance beams. The canal then runs along by the large and impressive Marsworth reservoirs, now a bird sanctuary, though having been 'dive bombed' here by swallows, it is my conviction that what is needed is a people sanctuary. Marsworth is yet another vivid reminder of the importance of water-supply to the canals. The broad locks of the Grand Union use something like 254,000 litres (56,000 gallons), so that each boat going across the summit of the canal sends two lock-fulls or about 500,000 litres (112,000 gallons) on their way down and out of the system. Steadily, the canal now becomes more open, more removed from town and suburb. We are back with the familiar pleasures of locks with trim cottages, open fields, wooded cuts and views of distant hills. There are a few intrusions into the peace, as at Wolverton, but here there is compensation in the Wolverton aqueduct, built in cast iron to replace the original that burst its brick walls in 1808. A short distance further on is Cosgrove with a quite extraordinary gothic bridge, not a style of building one associates with canals. The canal climbs again towards the busiest spot on the waterways, Stoke Bruerne. This appears to have been put together with picture postcards in mind: the white double-arched bridge, the cottages gay with mementoes of the working boats, the thatched pub and the old warehouse now converted to the Waterways Museum. Throughout the year it is crowded with visitors.

For those who do not like crowds, certain escape is not far away—the 2794 m (3056 yd) of Blisworth tunnel, which is wide enough for boats to pass. All kinds of propulsion have been used for boats at Blisworth: they have been legged through, shafted through and pulled through by steam-tugs at various times in the tunnel's history. Out in the light again, the canal is back in agricultural country, where the uneven ground forces it into a somewhat winding route, during which it receives a number of visits from the M1. At Braunston we are back at the Oxford Canal, and Braunston Junction is a much favoured canal meeting-place, marked or marred, depending on your point of view, by the large *Rose and Castle* pub, with its pseudo-paddle-boat bar.

North-west from Braunston, the canal pushes on to the heart of the Midlands. At first the landscape is empty, but the towns get nearer and the locks become steadily more frequent, a flight of eleven at Stockton being the first indication of what is to come. The first large town is Leamington, the Royal Spa that was once the Midlands' answer to Bath. But the canal whisks through with hardly a glance, content to stay in its own deep cutting before swinging away to neighbouring Warwick. Then comes one of the really grand, if daunting, sights of the canals—Hatton flight, twenty-one wide locks in stately procession up the hillside. Where some flights remain almost hidden in bends and slopes, Hatton stretches out before you in its entirety. The route passes close to Birmingham, but there is little hint of it in the fine canal scenery; only when the long cutting through Solihull finally ends does the city really take over for the remainder of the journey, where factories, offices and the vast piers of the motorway dominate the view.

The Grand Union is not just its main line, and one arm at least deserves special mention, the Leicester Arm. It is a continually pleasant route and offers, at Foxton, a unique double staircase of locks. The canal at this point rises through two five-lock staircases, separated only by a very short pound to allow boats to pass. Close by is one of the canal's notable failures, the Foxton inclined plane. It was built at the beginning of the century to bypass these troublesome locks, ran for eleven years, and was closed again because it was too expensive. The lines of the tracks, along which the giant caissons with their narrow boats floating inside once travelled up and down, are all that remain. Past Foxton another arm turns off towards Market Harborough, a busy canal base where narrow boats for the pleasure trade are now built and hired out. The Leicester Arm itself continues on its rural way to Leicester, where it undergoes a startling change of character. Suddenly we are in the world of factory and mill as the textile industry dominates the banks. For those who are interested it is a fascinating area and some of the mills are remarkably handsome, and none more so than the Donisthorpe factory, with its charming cupola and weather vane. The route can then be continued on until one joins up with the river Trent between Nottingham and Shardlow.

Length—from Limehouse to Digbeth Junction: 243 km (151½ miles); 140 locks.

Brecon and Abergavenny Canal

We now move from the English Midlands to a short, isolated route in South Wales, but one which offers scenery that can hardly be rivalled. Indeed, the whole of its course is run through the Brecon Beacons National Park. Not surprisingly in such mountainous country, the canal is forced to twist and turn, but by clinging to the hillsides it is able to complete the whole of its 53 km (33 miles) journey with only six locks to negotiate.

Starting at the southern end of the navigation at Pontypool, the canal gets off to a calm start, winding along as the mountains that flank it to the west begin to rise ever higher, while the valley, broadening in wide vistas to the east, is only closed from view where the woods come down the hillside. It is difficult today to imagine why such a canal was ever built, but a stop at a wharf area, such as that of Llanfoist, can provide the answer. At first view it is just one more beautiful reach, the high, wooded hillside to the west, the town of Abergavenny far below in the valley. Here, however, is a very extensive wharf with a large, wharf manager's house and a two-storey warehouse. If you take time off to explore you will find unmistakable signs of a tramway siding, and pursuing the matter further you can find a well-defined track leading up through the hillside woods. If you are energetic enough to walk up the hill you will find many of the stone tramway sleepers and even sections of rail, and a really long walk will eventually bring you to the now ruined ironworks that brought the canal into being.

For those whose only wish is to dawdle along this lovely canal there is the continuing delight of hills and woods and, in early summer, the banks are bright with rhododendrons. There are many canal pleasures to be had, including a short tunnel at Ashford and a most attractive four-arched aqueduct over the river Usk. One new addition is the lift bridge at Talybont, built to replace a low bridge that had made navigation impossible. The Brecon Canal is a very gentle one, but it offers so much to see along the route that even dedicated canal travellers are happy, for once, to get off the boat and on to dry land.

Length 53 km (33 miles); 6 locks.

Caledonian Canal

A mighty leap in more ways than one: from the Welsh hills to the Scottish Highlands, from narrow meanderings to great deep channels, from canal boat to seagoing vessel. The Caledonian is a ship-canal, cutting across the centre of Scotland from Fort William in the west to Inverness in the east and made up partly of artificial cutting and partly of the natural waters of the lochs Lochy, Oich and Ness. Among its many distinctions, the Caledonian can thus claim to be the only canal to boast its own monster. Apart from the possibilities of meeting that elusive creature the route offers a mixture between canal travel and cruising on the wide expanses of the deep lochs.

No canal could ask for a more spectacular beginning than the Caledonian receives at its western end. There, with Ben Nevis in the background, the waterway begins almost immediately to climb up through the great locks known as Neptune's Staircase. The poet Southey described the locks as Britain's 'greatest work of art' and compared them with the Pyramids, to the detriment of the latter. Even if not going quite so far as Southey, one cannot help admiring this great feat of civil engineering, completed a century and a half ago. The canal continues down the glen to Loch Lochy and, as is true throughout the journey, the scenery is dominated by the hills of the Highlands. The next artificial section might seem a little tame, for the country flattens out slightly and the canal runs straight on its course, bounded by pines. Yet as a work of engineering this is one of the greatest achievements of the canal age, greater even than Neptune's Staircase. For here we are in the very deepest of cuttings, where once railways were laid, steam-dredgers worked and thousands of men laboured at the barrow-runs. This is the Laggan Cut and it ends in natural waters before another section, closely following the line of the river Oich, takes us into the long narrow deeps of Loch Ness.

The final section of the canal carries us on towards the Beauly Firth at Clachnaharry, where the last of the engineering marvels on this great canal can be found. In order to give access to the canal at all states of the tide, Telford built his canal out into the waters of the Firth itself on a huge clay embankment, inside which he constructed the masonry walls of the sea-lock. When the great oak gates of the lock were hung they were 365 m (400 yds) out from the shore line.

Pleasure-boats are available on the canal, though it is mainly used by fishing-vessels. It is unique, quite unlike anything to be found in the rest of the British canal system and those who know the Highlands will need no further recommendation of the canal's attractions.

Overall length 97·3 km (60½ miles); 28 locks.

Crinan Canal

This again is a ship canal, though really only for use by seagoing vessels who want to avoid the 137 km (85 mile) passage round the Mull of Kintyre by taking this short 15 km (9 mile) cut. Though short, it is hardly less spectacular than the Caledonian, and shows in its rocky cuttings the immense problems faced by its engineers.

Canals for restoration

The growth of interest in canals has led to a steadily growing movement towards restoring derelict canals. Some that have been restored have been mentioned already, work on others is in progress and yet more are simply dreams for the future. To end these canal profiles, it seemed appropriate to include some notes on these routes, and even if when this book reachers the reader's hands the canals are still not open for traffic they can still provide pleasant walks. Better still, the reader might be tempted to join the ranks of the amateur navvies.

Kennet and Avon Canal Restoration

The Kennet and Avon is by far the most ambitious scheme of restoration yet to be tackled and already some considerable lengths are open for navigation. When work is finally completed it will be one of the most attractive and popular of routes.

The canal is, strictly speaking, three quite different waterways: the Kennet Navigation joining Reading to Newbury, the Kennet and Avon itself from Newbury to Bath, and the Avon from Bath to Bristol.

A lovely route, the Kennet and Avon gets off to an unlovely start by the Thames-side gasworks in Reading. The Navigation is a mixture of natural river and artificial cuts, perhaps best-known for having strange turf-sided locks. Once safely clear of the gasworks, the Kennet provides a pleasant introduction to the canal itself. At Newbury, the navigation passes the old town wharf, now a lorry park, then goes under a pleasant ornamental bridge in the centre of the town to meet the first lock of the canal. This is a beautiful site, dominated by the tall tower of the fifteenth-century church, and the canal itself is lined with rather grand houses that date back to the time when Newbury was a prosperous wool town. Unlike the Kennet Navigation, the canal itself could hardly have a more auspicious beginning. Once it leaves the town it is set on a journey of many kilometres past swelling hills and wooded slopes and there is only the occasional train on a nearby railway to disturb the peace. The names of bridges and other spots along the canal reflect its mood: Oak Hill Down, Beech Tree Walk, Heathy Close and Honey Street. There is nothing here, however, to prepare one for the canal spectacular to be met at the next large town.

The passage through Devizes is not particularly interesting or exciting, but once out on the western side the canal swoops down the hill in the great Caen Hill flight. Twenty-nine broad locks there are here, and to keep them fed with water a whole series of ponds have been terraced into the hillside. Now all are derelict and decayed, but one day the canal will again have to cope with Caen Hill if the navigation is to be restored. It is a sobering thought.

West of Caen Hill, the canal has reached the heart of the once prosperous woollen industry of Wiltshire and Somerset, and its major centres such as Bradford-on-Avon and Trowbridge. Bradford is now better known as a tourist centre and beauty spot; it is difficult to imagine that its woollen industry was once more important than that of its Yorkshire namesake. Beyond the town, the canal crosses the river on the first of the two great aqueducts, that proclaim at once in their finely proportioned classical styling that they are the work of John Rennie. This is Avoncliff, and looking down on the river you can see a large weir, at either end of which are woollen-mills, one of which still retains its water-wheel.

Now the Avon valley begins to close in and the scenery becomes, if anything, even more attractive. To complete the scene is the second of the aqueducts, the Dundas. In spite of some rather clumsy patching of the stonework, Dundas ranks second only to Rennie's Lune aqueduct as a piece of classical styling, and its elegance is enhanced by the lovely honey-coloured Bath stone of which it is built. It serves as a fitting introduction to the final run towards that most stylish of cities, Bath. Here too, although now apparently so remote from any industrial connections, is the spot where the Kennet and Avon joined the now vanished Somerset Coal Canal. But on down the valley, past the sweeping bend of Bathampton and Bath itself is in view, its terraces piled up the hillside. The canal, however, meets Bath's challenge with aplomb. At Sidney Gardens, the bridges are consciously styled to fit into the townscape created by John Wood and his successors, echoing the two characteristic themes of classical stonework and decorative iron. Even such an apparently mundane object as the engine-house at Widcombe locks seems to have been imbued with the Georgian genius for right proportions.

The route now continues by the river Avon, but the canal itself ends here with some splendour.

Restorations Probable and Possible

The Kennet and Avon, being partly open, deserves its due allowance of space, and even if unused its two aqueducts and the Caen Hill flight would ensure it a worthy place among canals. Other canals are, at the time of writing, unusable but in some cases there is real hope that they will be restored.

The Montgomery Canal, which leads southwards from the Llangollen Canal at Frankton Junction, west of Ellesmere, is scheduled for eventual reopening. An almost entirely rural canal it begins quietly enough, making its way through flat or gently rolling pastures and arable farmland. But once it crosses the Vyrnwy river, which it does by a low, four-arched aqueduct, the Welsh hills become steadily more dominant on the western flank, though the east still gives wide views across the Severn valley. At Welshpool the eastern view, too, closes in so that by the end of the journey at Newtown, the canal has undergone a complete transformation from the placid scenery of its beginning to the dramatic hill scenery at its end.

Two northern waterways deserve special mention, though in both cases their restoration would involve overcoming some awesome obstacles. The Rochdale and Huddersfield Canals are both trans-

Pennine routes, and are every bit as exciting as their geography woul
suggest. The Huddersfield perhaps gets the worst of the scenic bargain
since it goes through rather than over the hills, by way of Standedg
tunnel, which at almost exactly 3·2 km (2 miles) is the longest in th
country. It is also, according to those who have travelled it, the mos
unpleasant, for the railway tunnel runs next to it, and the fumes seep in
Apparently, in the days of steam-engines, the boatmen were very fortunate if they did not emerge from Standedge half choked and black wit
soot. Nevertheless, tunnel apart, the canal offers splendid views of hill
and moors, and gives a historical tour of the textile industry, passin
everything from the old hand-loom weavers' cottages to steam-mills an
modern factories. The Rochdale offers scenery even more spectacula
than the Huddersfield, winding its way through narrow valleys o
running through cuts blasted out of the hard Pennine rock. Like th
Huddersfield, it is a historian's paradise. It also offers at Sowerb
bridge, where it joins the Calder and Hebble Navigation, a group o
warehouses with covered bays which, now that Ellesmere Port has gone
is the best example in the country.

Two other canals that feature long tunnels have fallen into decay
The Basingstoke Canal has the 1097·3 m (1200 yds) long Greywel
which collapsed in 1932, and the scene round the tunnel is now mor
like a jungle than a navigation. Many sectors, however, are still i
water, and plans are in hand to bring it back into use. But the Thame
and Severn has gone, one fears, for ever, although there is so much o
interest to see just by walking along its course, that it is well wort
visiting. Sapperton tunnel was the canal's greatest engineering feature
and one should also look out for the unusual circular lock-cottages an
the often surprisingly well-preserved warehouses, left behind long afte
all traces of the canal have disappeared.

Some canals have left few traces, others, though unusable, are sur
prisingly well-preserved. Space prohibits mentioning them all, and fo
those whose personal favourites have been omitted, one can do no mor
than offer apologies.

Individual Sites

Not everyone can take weeks to explore canals, but there are a numbe
of sites around the country which are themselves of special interest an
which can be visited on a day's outing.

The Waterways Museum at Stoke Bruerne is an obvious starting
place for anyone wanting a first look at the world of the canals. In th

museum is a fascinating mixture of old prints and photographs, documents, notices and posters; there are models of engineering works such as Anderton lift; the whole of the stern section of a narrow boat can be seen, its cabin furnished in traditional style. Perhaps the most impressive thing about Stoke Bruerne is that the museum is so closely integrated into the canal scene: among the photographs on the museum walls is one of a group of boat families dressed up for a christening in 1913, and if you look out of the window you can see the place where the photograph was taken, hardly changed with the years.

There is usually a bustle of activity at the busy locks outside the Stoke Bruerne museum. At Crofton, near Great Bedwyn on the Kennet and Avon Canal, the excitement and activity is indoors. Here is a pumping-station where water is taken from Wilton Water, a small lake beside the canal, and pumped away along a feeder channel to the top of the Crofton flight of locks. What is so remarkable about Crofton is the pair of engines installed to do the work. These are steam-engines, and thanks to the care and enthusiasm of volunteers they are kept in full working order. One was built in 1845 by the famous Cornish engine-builders, Harveys of Hayle, and the other was built in 1812 by the even more famous firm of Boulton and Watt. The latter engine, which began its working life during the Napoleonic Wars, is the world's oldest working steam-engine, and to see it get under way, the huge iron beam slowly and ponderously rocking backwards and forwards is a uniquely exciting experience, for the beam is 8·8 m (29 ft) long and weighs 6 tons. The amount of water shifted at each stroke is a revelation and it is no surprise to see the enormous boilers needed to feed these two powerful, nodding giants. The engines can be seen every weekend, but they are only worked on special steaming weekends. These are widely advertised and details can always be obtained from the Kennet and Avon Trust.

Further along the same canal at Claverton is another pumping-station, where restoration work is well under way and which should be open to the public by late 1974. Here, too, a beam pump is used to lift water, in this case from the river Avon to the canal, but instead of using the power of steam, the power of the river itself is used. The water from the river turns a water-wheel which works the pumps—the power of the water lifts the water, a job well done and without fuel costs.

A new development in the scope of museums has been seen in recent years with the opening of a number of industrial museums, some of which have canal exhibits. Of these the most impressive and important is the open air museum at Blists Hill, near Ironbridge in Shropshire. The museum was designed round a number of existing features, notably the ironworks for which the area is famous, but including the Shropshire Tub-boat Canal, which has been cleared and restored. This little canal winds round the hill and ends in a steep inclined plane, the Hay incline, which took the tub-boats down to Coalport and the lower level of the canal beside the Severn.

Other remains of inclined planes can be seen. At Morwellham in the West Country, on the banks of the Tamar, the incline joined the once busy harbour to the Tavistock Canal. The canal itself was built to serve the neighbouring tin and copper mines, and a short distance from the top of the incline is the Tavistock tunnel. It has a surprisingly small entrance, but the work in building it was immense, for most of it had to be blasted through the solid rock. A different kind of canal-incline connection can be seen in Derbyshire near Cromford, where the canal built to serve Arkwright's cotton empire, meets the Cromford and High Peak Railway—the same railway that ends eventually in a meeting with the Peak Forest Canal at Whaley Bridge.

One other museum must be mentioned. At Cheddleton, on the Caldon branch of the Trent and Mersey, there are two water-powered flint mills where the flints for use in pottery glazes were ground. This is a doubly interesting site for canal enthusiasts. Firstly, it is fascinating in the way in which the wharf itself has been used as part of the actual process, for kilns have been built into the stone-work so that boats could unload directly into the top of the chambers. Secondly, the machinery of the mill, which is all in working order, was almost certainly built by none other than James Brindley, wearing, as it were, his millwright's rather than his canal-engineer's hat.

There are many, many more things to see and places to investigate than one could possibly list in a short book. Indeed, there are probably many more than any one person knows about. All one can say is that a visit to a canal, whether by boat or on foot, always provides a new experience, a new glimpse into the working life of what was once the nation's greatest transport system.

'URTHER READING

:he main guide books for the canal traveller are *Nicholson's Guides to the Vaterways*, five volumes that cover the main canals of England and Vales, but not those in Scotland.

;eneral Interest

)oerflinger, Frederic, *Slow Boat Through England*, Allan Wingate, 1970

;agg, John, *Canals in Camera*, Ian Allan, 1971

Iadfield, Charles, *The Canal Enthusiast's Handbook*, David and Charles (published at regular intervals)

Iadfield, Charles and Streat, Michael, *Holiday Cruising on Inland Waterways*, David and Charles, 1971

Iarris, Robert, *Canals and their Architecture*, Hugh Evelyn, 1969

AcKnight, Hugh, *Canal and River Craft in Pictures*, David and Charles, 1969

Rolt, L. T. C., *The Inland Waterways of England*, Allen and Unwin, 1950

:hurston, Temple, *The Flower of Gloster*, David and Charles, 1972

'anal History

iurton, Anthony, *The Canal Builders*, Eyre Methuen, 1972

;ladwin, D. D. and White, J. M., *English Canals* (three vols), Oakwood Press, 1968

Iadfield, Charles, *The Canal Age*, David and Charles; Pan Books, 1968

—— *British Canals*, David and Charles, 1960

Rolt, L. T. C., *Navigable Waterways*, Longmans, 1969

mith, Peter, *Waterways Heritage*, Luton Museum, 1971

For those who want more detailed works, there are a number of eprints of canal classics of the nineteenth century now available, and *'anals of the British Isles* (David and Charles,), under the editorship f Charles Hadfield, is a complete history (in several volumes) of all ritish canals. There are also several biographies of canal engineers and ther canal personalities.

INDEX

Figures in bold type refer to plate numbers

SISTERS

Also by Lily Tuck

The Double Life of Liliane

The House at Belle Fontaine

I Married You for Happiness

Woman of Rome: A Life of Elsa Morante

The News from Paraguay

Limbo, and Other Places I Have Lived

Siam: or, The Woman Who Shot a Man

The Woman Who Walked on Water

Interviewing Matisse: or, The Woman Who Died Standing Up

SISTERS

A NOVEL

LILY TUCK

Atlantic Monthly Press
New York

Published simultaneously in Canada
Printed in the United States of America

FIRST EDITION

ISBN 978-0-8021-2711-2
eISBN 978-0-8021-8920-2

Atlantic Monthly Press
an imprint of Grove Atlantic
154 West 14th Street
New York, NY 10011

Distributed by Publishers Group West

groveatlantic.com

17 18 19 20 10 9 8 7 6 5 4 3 2 1

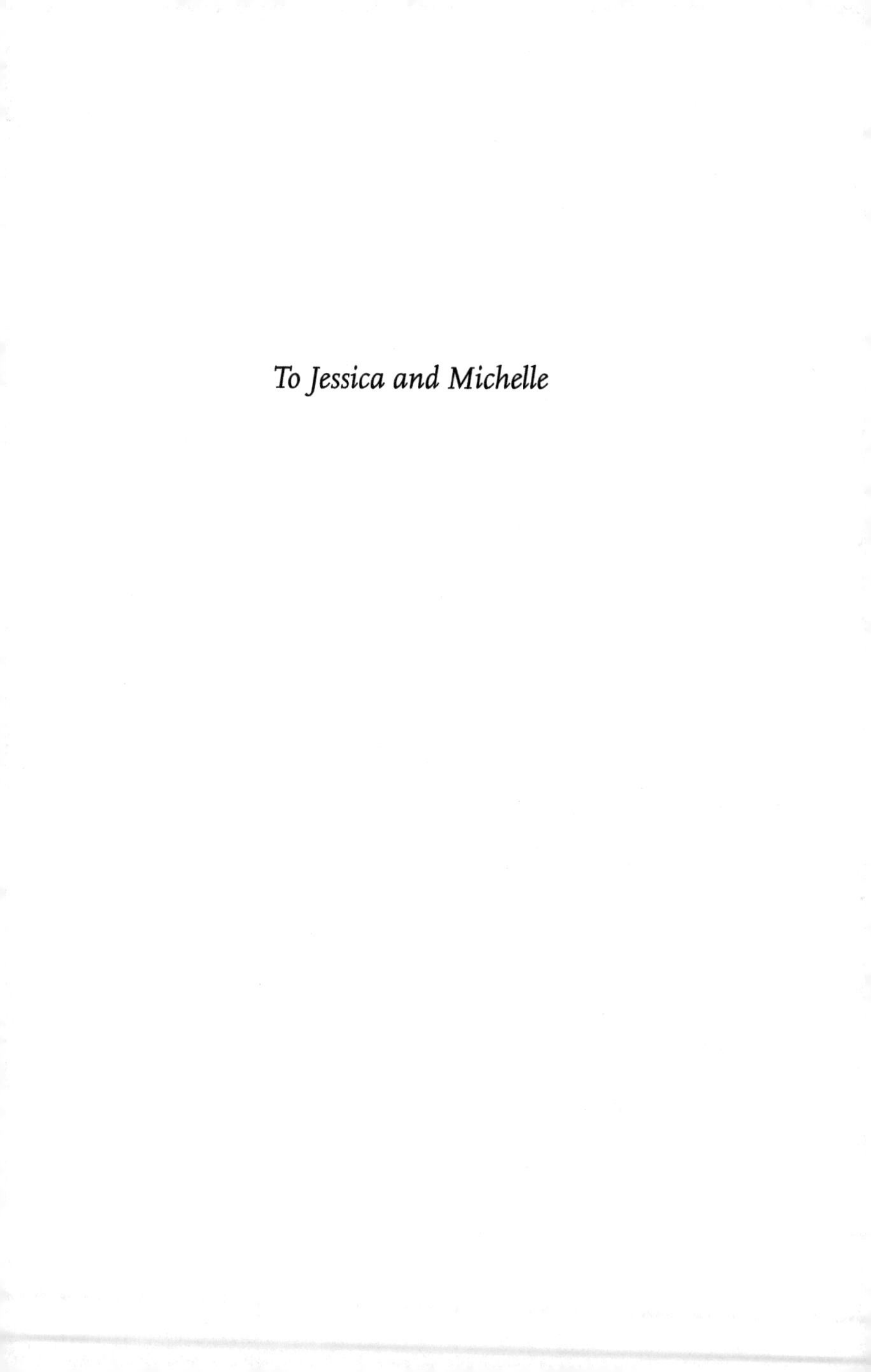

To Jessica and Michelle

First and second wives are like sisters.

—Christopher Nicholson (*Winter*)

SISTERS

We are not related—not remotely.

In the old days it was not unusual for a man, after his wife had died—but *she* is not dead—to marry his wife's younger sister. Already she had come into the household to care for her dying sister and then remained to care for the children, do the cooking and the housework. She was a useful and necessary presence. Think of Charles Austen, Jane Austen's brother, think of the painters William Holman Hunt and John Collier; all three married their dead wives' sisters despite the fact that until 1907 there was a ban in England, the Deceased Wife's Sister Marriage Act, on such marriages—known as sororate marriages. In the Hebrew Bible, Jacob's marriage to the sisters Rachel and Leah, forebears of the Twelve Tribes of Israel, is also such an example.

And we don't look alike. *She* is blond, fair-skinned, big-boned, and taller than I. I have also seen photos of her as a young woman and I have to admit *she* was lovely. Truly. Now, *she* is a handsome woman in a slightly ravaged way. Her best feature is her nose—a Grecian nose, I think they call it—the sort that has no bridge and starts straight from the forehead. Like Michelangelo's *David*.

I am dark and petite.

According to Wikipedia, Michelangelo's *David* is 5.16 meters or nearly 17 feet tall and weighs 5,660 kilos or 12,478.12 pounds.

In one of the photos I saw of her as a young woman, *she* is pushing a baby carriage—an old-fashioned big black baby carriage—down a city street in Paris. The street is shaded by large chestnut trees and, in addition to pushing the carriage, *she* is holding a little dog on a leash. The dog, a white-and-black terrier, is straining at the leash.

"Heel," *she* could be telling the dog. "Heel, damn it," but the dog pays her no attention.

"She didn't like dogs much," my husband once told me. "She liked cats. I hate cats," he adds.

"I love dogs," I told my husband.

At first I had pictured her in a house full of cats. Cats everywhere. Cats stretched out on the sofa, on the chairs, lying on top of the kitchen table, sitting on the windowsill licking themselves clean, eating from bowls on the floor. A mess. I was reminded of the book I had just read about poor Camille Claudel, Rodin's discarded mistress, made mad by neglect and poverty. Her apartment on the Quai de Bourbon in Paris, a home for feral cats.

Sometimes when I could not sleep—many nights, actually; I have insomnia—instead of counting sheep, I tried to count the number of times during their marriage that they had made love. I was just guessing of course but, for argument's sake, let's say that for the first two years—they were both young, in their twenties—they made love nearly every night so call that one thousand fucks; then the third and fourth year, maybe they made love only two or three times a week so let's call that three hundred fucks and then, of course, it got less. Also, *she* had had two kids in between, so again, if they made love two or three times a week for the next eight or nine years that made it about eight hundred more fucks and, probably, toward the end of their marriage, they didn't fuck at all. So I was guessing that *she* and my husband fucked about two thousand times during their marriage. As for me and my husband—we were older, he was in his forties—we fucked a lot the first year and after that we fucked only once or twice a week and usually only on Sunday mornings.

I was told that *she* was musical. I was also told—by the same person, a person who knew her quite well before her marriage, a fellow student, in fact—that *she* could have had a career as a concert pianist. *She* spent two years in Philadelphia studying at the Curtis Institute of Music, which has one of the most competitive and storied piano performance departments in the world.

"I remember how she said she would never forget studying with Eleanor Sokoloff and Seymour Lipkin—especially Seymour Lipkin," the same person who knew her quite well told me. "And how Lipkin told her that as a pianist she had a moral responsibility to the composer to play what the composer thought and felt and not what she felt like playing. She told me she would never forget that. Funnily enough," the person said, "I haven't forgotten that either."

Once married, however, *she* gave it up.

Did he dissuade her? I wondered.

I have a career, but I am not a pianist or an artist. My career gives me some financial freedom, it gets me out of the house, but it is not all consuming. If I had to give it up tomorrow, it would not matter much. I am not passionate about my work.

I also could not help wondering if *she* resented him for making her give up her career—if that is what he did or if that is what he, in his most charming and persuasive way, suggested.

And did her resentment contribute to their getting divorced? My guess is that the reason they got divorced was not due entirely to her giving up the piano.

I also have to say here that as far as music is concerned I have a tin ear.

"She and I took lessons with Mrs. Sokoloff on her Bösendorfer," the fellow student who had known her added.

"Her what?"

"A Bösendorfer piano has ninety-seven keys instead of eighty-eight. The extra nine keys are at the bass end of the keyboard, and on Mrs. Sokoloff's piano they were hidden underneath a hinged panel mounted between the piano's conventional low A and the left-hand end cheek so that you would not accidentally hit them. Now, instead of concealed by a panel, the extra keys are painted black to differentiate them from the standard eighty-eight."

As for her children—a boy and a girl—we get along now. But when their father and I first married, I had worried. I was nervous. The boy, thirteen at the time, seemed indifferent to me. The girl, slightly older, was hostile. Not having children of my own, I tried too hard to please them. I wanted them to like me—to love me—and I allowed them liberties that, in retrospect, I should not have. For instance, I never said anything when they did not make their beds or when they threw their wet towels on the floor in the bathroom. I also did not say anything when they left their dirty dishes for me to take to the sink and wash. As time passed, however, I relaxed and acted more honestly. I spoke my mind.

I think they eventually understood that instead of trying to replace their mother, I was supporting her.

Unfortunately, the boy got into drugs for a while. Looking back, I should perhaps have said something to him, but at the time I did not want to interfere.

"Does your mother have a cat?" I asked him once.

High, his pupils dark and dilated, he laughed.

"*Meow, meow.*"

I asked his daughter the same thing.

"She had two—Simone and Nelson. Unfortunately, Nelson, named for Nelson Algren, died last week. She's still very upset."

Nelson Algren famously wrote: *Never sleep with a woman whose troubles are worse than your own.*

People, of course, took sides. A lot of them blamed my husband for the divorce and some of them probably blamed me as well. But their blame was not justified. I had nothing to do with the divorce. Yes, it was true that I had met him while he was still married, but by then he and his wife were not getting along. In fact, as he later confessed to me, he and his wife had not had sex in over six months.

We met at a friend's dinner party and I remember how he told the hostess that he was very sorry but his wife had suddenly been taken sick with the flu and could not attend, although, as it turned out, the part about his wife being sick was not true. They had argued and at the last minute she said she was not going out for dinner and was staying home. As a result, the dinner party hostess had had to change the table seating at the last minute and I ended up sitting next to my future husband. The host was sitting on my other side and since I had known him since our college days I remember I did not feel intimidated or nervous. I even remember what I talked to the host about: we talked about how another classmate had moved to Silicon Valley and how neither one of us, no matter how financially beneficial that job might be, would ever want to do that. I actually have quite a good memory, or so I have been told, and I also remember what I was wearing—a pair of black tuxedo trousers (the kind with a satin stripe down the side) and a white silk blouse with a V-neck—and I can remember exactly what we ate at that dinner party: smoked salmon on toast to start with, then duck à l'orange, wild rice, and French string beans, then salad with assorted cheeses, and a crème brûlée for dessert. All of it delicious.

Preheat oven to 300 degrees.

In a small saucepan, combine cream, vanilla bean, and granulated sugar; place over medium heat and stir occasionally, until bubbles start to form around the edges of the pan. Do not boil. Remove from heat and set aside.

Whisk egg yolks in a large bowl; while whisking constantly, slowly add hot cream mixture to egg yolks. Continue whisking until—

But I promised myself never to copy down a recipe.

The last time I saw her was at her daughter's wedding, a grand affair for which my husband paid a small fortune. He was happy to and money never mattered much to him, for which I admired him; also, he liked his about-to-be new son-in-law. So did I. The wedding was formal—caterers, flowers, printed invitations—and a success. The reception took place at an elegant club in midtown and my guess was that there were over two hundred guests—most of them young and most of them his daughter's friends, which was as it should be. My husband wore his best blue suit, a white silk shirt, and a silver tie while I had gone out and bought a new dress. An expensive, designer navy polka-dot silk dress on which I got many compliments—even my husband said: "*Très chic!*" More important, his daughter looked beautiful. Since her father had offered to pay for the dress, we had gone together to several bridal boutiques and after many hesitations and concerns, on her part, she had finally chosen a beautiful satin gown with a pannier skirt—at least that was how the saleslady described it. The gown, I remember, had a series of—maybe thirty in all—tiny silk-covered buttons up the back and when she had tried it on, I had done them up for her. Not easy. On the day of the wedding, I imagined how her mother had had to do up all those buttons for her daughter.

During the dinner, while we were all sitting at our respective tables (I was seated, not at the head table with the bride and groom and my husband, but at an adjacent table with relatives—the aunts and uncles—of the groom), and after the toasts, there was music and dancing. My husband first danced with his daughter—after she had danced to Frank Sinatra's "Fly Me to the Moon" with the groom—and it made me happy to watch them. I know how much he loved his daughter. Next, he danced with his former wife and, to be honest, my heart sank as I watched them glide across the floor effortlessly to Frankie Valli's "Can't Take My Eyes Off of You." My husband was holding her tightly around the waist and *she* had her hand high up on his back, nearly touching his neck. I had to admit to myself that they looked good together. Eventually the groom's uncle who was sitting next to me and who had traveled all the way from Madison, Wisconsin, for the wedding, had asked me to dance.

Our own wedding was small. My sister and her husband came from Austin, Texas. Eloise and Harold. Eloise is a few years younger than I am and we have never been close. Less so once she got married and she had kids, reasons I suppose for her to act superior to me. I've met her kids. Her kids are surly and overweight.

We had dinner together the night before the wedding. My husband had booked a table for us at an expensive French restaurant and I noticed how Eloise took obvious greedy pleasure in her food—since I last saw her, she too had gained weight—and Harold seemed to be enjoying several glasses of wine, a Mouton Rothschild. But while we were waiting for our dessert—Eloise had ordered the tarte tatin—she followed me into the ladies' room and voiced her objections.

"He's divorced," she said.

"I know he's divorced," I answered from the adjoining stall.

"He might not be suitable," she said.
"Suitable how?" I asked, flushing the toilet.
"He's got two teenage kids."
"So? They have a mother."
"Have you met the mother?"
"Yes," I lied as I washed my hands.
"What is she like?"
"She's very nice."

I was in several relationships before I married my husband. Two of them serious. The first was in graduate school with a man named Tim. Tim and I were both getting our master's in communications at Tulane University; he wanted to go into television and I was not sure what I wanted—marketing, I said. We rented a house with some other students in the Garden District of New Orleans. We drank a lot, smoked pot, did a bit of cocaine, and collected beads at Mardi Gras. I can't remember why we broke up—we just did, and I moved back East. I was on my own for a while, I had a good job marketing tea and soups for a large Dutch company, and eventually I started going out with my boss. Of course, my boss was married and it was all tricky and difficult especially since I fell in love with him. Mostly we met on business trips to Amsterdam, where we would stay in the same hotel but book separate rooms. It was lovely and romantic until his wife found out. Someone in the office must have suspected and told her. She threatened to divorce him and he had to swear to her never to see me again which he did and which broke my heart.

I never told my husband any of this. And despite my own reservations about speaking of it, I have to admit that his lack of curiosity about my love life was not flattering.

Once while we were making love, my husband called out her name instead of mine.

Sometimes I wondered whether *she* had had boyfriends before they got married. Or was she still a virgin? I also wondered whether men find deflowering a woman for the first time thrilling and satisfying. Or do they think it an onerous task?

I should have asked him but didn't.

He had good taste and dressed well—he wore bespoke shirts made in England. And I liked how he smelled. A lot of men I have known have a sour smell, especially during sex. I liked that he could make me laugh—like the time we sat in my backyard garden and he said he felt as if he were in Holland.

Before we got married, he sent me flowers every single day.

The first time I saw her was from the living room window. *She* had bicycled over to our apartment with her daughter. *She* wore a long paisley skirt and wooden clogs.

"Was that your mother?" I asked her daughter, although I knew it was.

Somewhere I read that either alder, birch, sycamore, willow, or beech—woods that won't split—is chiefly used to make clogs.

I don't know why but I have been trying to think of his daughter's husband's uncle's name—the man I danced with at her wedding. I actually danced with him several times and each time he became more and more unruly. First he had put his hand on my butt, then he had tried to kiss me on the mouth right there in the middle of the dance floor. He must have been drunk. It was embarrassing, but I don't think anyone noticed. My husband did not notice. The man's name was on the tip of my tongue. But what I remember most about the evening was how I had felt abandoned and insignificant.

"Did you ever hear her play?"

"Who?" my husband asked.

"Your wife—I mean your ex-wife," I answered.

"Of course," my husband said. "Of course, I heard her play. I've already told you she played beautifully. She could have had a career as a pianist."

After dinner, we were watching television in the den—a live broadcast of a musical evening at the White House. President Obama and his wife, Michelle, were sitting in the front row; they both looked happy. Stevie Wonder was playing "As" on the piano.

"What did she play?" I continued.

"Classical stuff—you know—Mozart, Beethoven, Bach, Chopin . . ."

"Oh, I love Chopin," I said.

"I thought you said you had a tin ear?"

"I do, but I like listening to music. I just can't tell specifics like what key things are in. I just . . ."

My husband looked at me and frowned. "The point is?" he asked.

"Music can transport me."

My husband snorted.

Stevie Wonder finished playing and, smiling, Obama and Michelle clapped wildly.

I imagined her sitting at a grand piano, the one with the nine extra keys, in a huge concert hall; *she* swayed a little as *she* played and as her feet pressed down on the pedals. Her arms were bare and her blond hair shone in the light. Next to her, attentive, a young man was turning the pages of the music score. When *she* finished the piece *she* stood up and took a bow. The audience clapped wildly. *She* smiled and put her hands together to her chest to acknowledge the audience. The audience continued clapping.

"Encore, encore," someone in the audience shouted. Others took up the shout. "Encore!"

My old boyfriend Tim sent me an e-mail saying he was coming to town and he hoped to see me and catch up. He suggested we get together for a cup of coffee.

Sure, I thought. Why not?

She and I spoke at her son's graduation. His school was located in a small, pretty New England town and the day before the graduation my husband and I drove up to the town from the city. It was getting late as we were driving on the Mass Turnpike—he was going eighty-five miles an hour and the speed limit was sixty-five miles an hour—and we got stopped by a state trooper and the state trooper gave my husband a ticket. The ticket cost over two hundred dollars and my husband was furious. But worse still, the trooper made him get out of the car and take a Breathalyzer test as well as walk a straight line with his hands behind his head counting from one hundred-and-one down to eighty-one backward and by odd numbers. Not only was my husband furious but he was humiliated, so much so that it ruined the weekend for him (no doubt for his son as well). During the entire next day while we were at his son's graduation, he kept telling everyone he spoke to—his son's teachers, the other parents, whoever would listen to him—about how unfair the speeding ticket was and how humiliating it was to have to take the Breathalyzer test and how he was going to speak to the Massachusetts state attorney who was a friend of his to make sure that the state trooper, whose name he had taken down, was going to spend the rest of his life regretting this. It was embarrassing.

He even told his ex-wife about the speeding ticket and I remember how *she* just smiled and shrugged.

One hundred-and-one, ninety-nine, ninety-seven, ninety-five, ninety-three . . .

Occasionally, on the weekends when her children were staying with my husband and me, *she* telephoned and asked to speak to one of them.

Usually I was the one who was home and who answered the phone.

"He's out," I would tell her.

"He's out with his dad."

I never said he's out with my husband.

Usually they were out biking—biking for miles up the Hudson—all three of them good-looking, coordinated, athletic.

She lived across the city from us. Maybe a mile or two as the crow flies and, as a result, our paths did not cross a lot. But once, because her son had left a book at our house and had called saying he needed it right away for class, I took the crosstown bus and went to her apartment. The building was a high-rise and had several entrances and it took me a while to find the right one. Her apartment was on the eleventh floor and when *she* opened the door for me I could see *she* was surprised to see me. I, too, must have stared at her, and probably *she* thought I was staring at her outfit—black tights and a white T-shirt—because *she* said, "I do tai chi."

Stupidly, I said, "Oh, I do yoga."

Standing in the doorway, I could see into the living room which was painted white and looked airy and uncluttered. The furniture consisted of a single sofa, a coffee table, a few chairs, and a grand piano along the far wall. Out of the living room window I could see the river and the New Jersey shore.

"Do you want to come in for a minute?" *she* asked.

And instead of saying "Yes," I got embarrassed and lied. "Thanks, I have to run," I said. "I have an appointment downtown."

I handed her the book and, without another word, I turned and left.

"I'm sorry about Nelson, your cat," I might have said.

On the bus, on my way to her apartment I had tried reading her son's book:

In mathematician Felix Klein's posthumously published memoir Development of Mathematics in the Nineteenth Century *(1926), Klein says of Hermann Grassmann that unlike "we academics [who] grow in strong competition with each other like a tree in the midst of a forest which must stay slender and rise above the others simply to exist and to conquer its portion of light and air, he who stands alone can grow on all sides."*

Grassmann's mathematics was outside the mainstream of thought; read by few, his great work, Die lineale Ausdehnungslehre (The Theory of Linear Extension, *1844*), *was described even by Klein as "almost unreadable." Yet this book, more philosophy than mathematics, for the first time proposed a system whereby space and the geometric components and descriptions could be extrapolated to other dimensions.*

His son was musical, too. He played the guitar and was in a rock band at school. (I know a lot of kids play the guitar and are in bands.) Maybe I felt sorry for him because his father was always hard on him—harder than he was on his sister.

"He's a late bloomer," I said.

"Don't give me that late bloomer shit." My husband started to get angry. He never liked being disagreed with.

"He's good at math." I tried again. "Programming and all that technical computer stuff."

My husband did not answer.

"Maybe you should try to talk to his mother," I said.

"About what?" my husband asked.

I didn't answer.

On a few occasions, making an excuse to myself—fresher organic produce, hard-to-find Italian virgin olive oil—I would again take the cross-town bus to shop in her neighborhood. I would go to Fairway, the big supermarket that was just a few blocks from her apartment. Slowly I would push my cart down the aisles and study the clementines in season, the avocados, the hydroponically grown tomatoes; or I would stand in front of the cheese counter as if trying to decide which kind to buy—the Camembert or the Roquefort?—hoping to catch a glimpse of her. Sometimes, I stood around for such a long time without buying anything that the person behind the counter would get impatient and ask: "Miss, can I help you with something?"

Once while I was standing in front of the salt-water tank watching the live lobsters inside it, I saw what I thought was her reflection in the glass.

"Hi," I said, turning around quickly and calling out her name.

Only it wasn't her, and the woman, who was blond but otherwise did not look like her, frowned at me and said, "Fuck you, too."

"Have you ever had bouillabaisse?" his daughter asked me during dinner one night.

"No—bouilla—what?"

"Bouillabaisse. It's a French soup prepared from fish stock and different kinds of fish and shellfish, like mussels and clams. It comes with a sauce made with cayenne, saffron, garlic—"

"The best bouillabaisse I ever had was in Marseille," my husband said, interrupting. "I went there with your mother during a holiday—*la Toussaint*—when I was at INSEAD. It was October, months before you were born," he added, winking at his daughter.

"My mother makes it occasionally—it's really good," his son said.

"I'll never forget the restaurant," my husband continued, "it was right on the harbor. The old port. Nothing fancy and full of locals. I wish I could remember the name of it. *Chez* someone . . ."

"My mother got the recipe from a Julia Child cookbook. She says it takes her all day to make it," his daughter said.

"I wonder if the restaurant is still there," my husband continued. "I would go back in a heartbeat.

"*Chez Maurice*!" he almost shouted. "That's the name of the restaurant. A miracle I remembered it."

My guess, only a few months pregnant, *she* threw up the bouillabaisse in the street next to the old port.

Next morning, first thing, I went to the bookstore around the corner from where we live and bought Julia Child's *Mastering the Art of French Cooking,* Volumes 1 and 2.

The fish Julia Child's suggests to use for a bouillabaisse are halibut, eel, winter flounder, hake, baby cod, small pollock, and lemon sole. Shellfish, she writes, are not necessary but add glamour and color to the soup.

One of the arguments my husband and I had was over a dog. I had seen an ad at our bookstore—the bookstore owners are animal lovers and their cat sits on a pile of best sellers all day. Right away I called and was told that all but one male had already been sold. "Please," I begged, "can you keep him for me for a few days while I check with my husband? My husband is out of the country on business," I lied.

"Poodles are very smart. They are the second-smartest breed of dog after the Australian sheep-dog," I said, trying to convince my husband. "And the kids, too, like dogs."

"Who's going to walk the dog?" my husband asked. "Who is going to pick up the shit?"

My husband traveled a lot on business. However, instead of going to Europe and to glamorous cities like Paris, London, and Berlin, he mostly traveled in the United States and Canada. He went to cities like Dallas and Houston and San Francisco and Seattle and to cities in the Midwest like Des Moines and Saint Louis. Usually, he was away only a day or two and often, when he returned home, he was tired and hungover.

"Those lousy hotels," he said. "I can never get enough sleep."

"All those client dinners," I said.

"And missing you," he said, putting his arms around me.

My husband genuinely liked women.

Every so often my husband talked in his sleep. Usually the words were incomprehensible or they made no sense. Or no sense to me.

Turn off the water! he once called out. *It's too hot, I tell you!*

In the morning, I questioned him.

"What were you dreaming about last night?" I asked. "You were yelling about the water being too hot."

He shrugged. "Too hot? I don't remember."

"Were you taking a shower in your dream?" I persisted.

"I told you I don't remember."

One night, he repeatedly called out a woman's name. Not her name. *Lena.*

"Who's Lena?" I asked him in the morning.

"Lena? I don't know any Lena."

After a moment, he said, "Lena Horne. Maybe I was dreaming about Lena Horne."

"I love the chicken masala and the vegetable samosas, the bread, too—what's it called—naan," I told his daughter.

We were sitting in an Indian restaurant waiting for her father.

"Dad is always late," his daughter said.

It was her birthday and we were celebrating it.

"One day, I want to go," I said. "To India, I mean."

"My mother wants to go to India, too," his daughter said. "She wants to go to the state of Tamil Nadu."

"Tamil Nadu?" I repeated as my husband rushed into the restaurant full of apologies for being late and keeping us waiting.

"What shall we order?" he said sitting down. "Something spicy—I like spicy Indian food. And happy birthday, darling," he added.

"You know what I didn't realize?" his daughter once said to me.

She and I get along well. Very often I feel as if she could be my daughter, too.

"No, what?"

We were sitting in the living room after dinner; her father and brother were watching television in the den. A basketball game. We heard them yell excitedly from time to time.

"I didn't realize that my mother was happier once she got divorced from Dad. She sort of came into her own."

"How could you tell?" I asked.

"Well, for one thing, she wants to travel and, for another, she started playing the piano again. She loves that."

"What are you two talking about?" my husband asked, coming into the room during the commercial.

"Nothing," we both said.

I dreamed—not that I went back to Manderley—that I was in a big city like Calcutta or Bombay in India. I was sweating and the streets were packed with people pushing and shoving and beggars, too, who clutched at my skirt and tugged at my arm and, in the dream, I became more and more frightened and at one point I started to run when all of sudden I saw her. *She* was dressed in a bright green sari and *she* had a red dot painted on her forehead. Relieved to see someone I knew who could perhaps help me, I called out her name, but *she* kept on walking as if *she* did not know who I was. Then I woke up.

In the morning, when I started to tell my husband about how I had had a dream that upset me—without mentioning her—he interrupted me, saying, "I can never remember my dreams."

In the dictionary I looked up the red dot worn by Hindu women called a *bindi*. Traditionally, it is worn by married women; widows are not allowed to wear red, but they can wear a black dot; young women can wear a *bindi* of any color except black. The *bindi* is known as the third eye chakra. Worn between the eyebrows, where the pineal gland lies, it is said to retain energy and concentration.

In addition to sleeping pills, I also kept Valium in my medicine cabinet. I rarely took the Valium—only if I went to the dentist or if I flew. But when I went to take a Valium—I was on my way to the dentist to have a cavity filled—I noticed that there were a lot fewer pills in the little vial than I remembered. Instead of about twenty pills, there were only six. How so? I wondered. The housekeeper, Margarita, would not have taken them—she speaks little English and I would be surprised if she knew what the generic name *diazepam* signified. If his daughter had wanted some Valium I am sure she would have asked me, which left his son. Valium, I know, is a helpful downer if you are high on drugs.

Margarita came to work for us after Dona left. Apparently, Dona had been working for my husband's family for years, ever since the children were little, and everyone, except me, loved Dona. Dona left soon after I moved in. She never actually confronted me with any problems, only I felt them. And a few times, I had to point out to her that the furniture was not polished properly—rings left on the tables—and once I found hairs on top of the drain in one of the shower stalls. I tried to be as diplomatic as possible but at the same time I had to assert myself. I also could not help wondering about what *she* was like as a housewife—did *she* not care that things were not clean and tidy? Then I found pieces of my grandmother's china sauceboat in the garbage. The sauceboat was part of a Meissen china collection my grandmother had brought over from Europe and given to me. Each cup, plate, and saucer as well as the sauceboat was decorated with little pastel flowers and each piece had the two blue crossed swords—the Meissen authenticity mark—incised in the back. Needless to say I was and am very fond of this china for both sentimental and aesthetic reasons, to say nothing of how valuable the china is. Anyway, I confronted Dona with the pieces and of course she denied breaking the sauceboat. The next week she told me she was leaving. Her excuse was that she had to babysit for her new grandchild. I paid her for an extra two weeks and let her go. Afterward I complained to my husband about Dona and told him about finding the broken pieces of the sauceboat in the garbage.

"I'm pretty sure she was lying," I told him.

"She wasn't," my husband said.

"How do you know?"

"I broke the sauceboat."

"What?"

"I was reaching for something on the shelf and it fell out. Sorry," he said. "And I didn't know you cared so much about it."

"I do and why didn't you tell me?" I asked, close to tears.

"I forgot," he said.

"I'll get you another," he added.

The other thing I remembered about his daughter's wedding—besides my husband dancing with his former wife and the groom's drunken uncle dancing with me—was running into her in the ladies' room. I was just coming out of a stall when *she* went into it—I remember holding the door open for her at the same time that we gave each other a little smile, a nervous little smile.

"Oh, hello," *she* said.

"Hello," I said back.

And those were the only two words we exchanged. However, looking back on this encounter, I can't help laughing at the thought of her sitting on the same toilet seat I had just vacated—only it should have been the other way around.

Ha ha.

Suspended for a term from his school for drinking alcohol, his son worked at the local public library.

"All I do is shelve books," he told me. "It's boring. I can't even read. When I graduate, I am going to travel—"

"If you graduate," his father interrupted, walking into the room.

"And don't you encourage him," he added, shaking his head at me.

“Congratulations,” I said to her. “You must be very proud.”

“A relief,” *she* answered with a slight smile. “I didn’t think he would make it all the way to graduation.”

The ceremony over, parents and students were standing together outside on the school’s manicured lawn.

“I did,” I said.

She looked at me without speaking.

“He’s a very intelligent and talented boy,” I said to fill in the silence. “I’m very fond of him,” I added since *she* still had not spoken.

“He’s fond of you, too,” *she* finally said.

"The majority of bond trading is done between institutions," my husband told us. At dinner, after a few glasses of wine, he was more loquacious and expansive and more apt to try to explain what he did all day. "And depending on the number of bonds being bought, the price can be negotiated."

"What about junk bonds?" his son asked.

"Junk bonds get a bad rap. Even if they have a credit rating below the BBB by Standard and Poor's because they have a higher risk of default they still will pay a higher interest rate. The right junk bond fund can be a smart move for a diversified portfolio."

"What about the mortgage-backed securities?" His daughter was more numerate than her brother and more up-to-date on the news.

My husband raised his eyebrows at her and said, "I can't believe you are really interested." Then before she could answer, he continued, "MBSs are bonds secured by home and other real estate loans.

They are created when a number of these loans are pooled together. For instance, a bank offering home mortgages might round up ten million dollars' worth of such mortgages. That pool is then sold to a federal government agency or a government-sponsored enterprise or to a securities firm. Another group called 'private label' MBSs are issued by subsidiaries of investment banks—like ours." He paused, poured himself more wine. "Unlike traditional fixed-income bonds, most MBSs give bondholders monthly—not semiannual—interest payments. The reason for this is that homeowners pay their mortgages monthly, not twice a year. The big difference between Treasury bonds and MBSs is that the Treasury bond pays you interest only, and at the end of the bond's maturity you get a lump-sum principal amount, while an MBS pays you both interest and principal. This of course means that when the MBS matures you don't get a lump-sum principal payment. Do you follow me?"

His daughter nodded while his son and I said nothing.

I was curious about the two years he studied at INSEAD—Institut européen d'administration des affaires. The school was located outside Paris in Fontainebleau and he had to commute from the small apartment they rented off Avenue Foch. (Avenue Foch must have been where the photo was taken of her pushing the baby carriage while holding the little terrier on the leash.)

"Did you learn to speak French?" I asked him.

"Enough French to order a meal and get around."

And what about her? My guess was that *she* picked up French in no time because *she* was musical and had a good ear.

Parlez-vous?

I have always wanted to go to Paris—France is a lot closer than India.

One time, my husband asked me to go with him to Montreal for a few days, but I could not go. I had already planned to meet Tim, my old boyfriend, for coffee that week.

By then, too, I had begun taking French lessons with Mademoiselle Millet on Tuesday afternoons. We sat in the dining room and for the first half hour we did grammar. Mademoiselle Millet was adamant about grammar, pronouns, verbs and their conjugation, and feminine and masculine nouns:

La table, le lit . . .

(A table, wooden and solid, should be masculine, a bed, soft and embracing, feminine . . .)

She was also adamant about pronunciation.

"*U*," she said, "*u, u, u.*"

"*Ou, ou,*" I repeated.

If I had gone to Montreal with my husband, I would have had the opportunity to practice my French and see the Rodin exhibit at the Musée des Beaux Arts. According to the museum's website, there were 300 works on loan from the Musée Rodin in Paris, which included the monumental plaster of *The Walking Man*—I watched an online video showing how the museum staff carefully uncrated and assembled the statue. In addition to *The Walking Man*, there were 171 sculptures, sketches, and watercolors, as well as seventy photographs by Eugène Druet in the show. I am especially interested in photography and consider myself a fairly good amateur photographer—before I got married, I saved my money to buy photographs and camera equipment. I would love to have seen those Druet photographs.

Rodin's sculptures reminded me again of poor Camille Claudel.

His daughter often spoke of her. She spoke of her mother in an ordinary way and not in a way to offend or annoy me.

For instance, at dinner one night, his daughter said, "Mom and I went to a movie the other day. We loved it. You should see it," she said turning to me. "The movie or I should say 'film' is Russian. I think it was made years ago—we saw it at Film Forum, where they show old movies. It takes place during World War II and it is incredibly sad. Also, there is this beautiful scene where Boris, the soldier, is shot and as he falls dying, he sees the birch trees turning and spinning above him and—"

"*The Cranes Are Flying,*" I said.

"You've seen it then."

"It's one of my favorite films," I told his daughter.

I suggested the park to his son. I suggested he take his bicycle and told him to ride around on it while I photographed him with my Rolleiflex 3.5 F. He was very coordinated and he liked to clown. One of the best photographs I took was of him standing with one foot on the seat and the other on the crossbar of his bicycle, his arms spread out, and laughing.

"I saw this film by Bertolucci," he told me afterward. "It's one of his earliest films, it's called *Before the Revolution*. Have you seen it?"

I shook my head.

"Anyway, it starts out with this blond guy standing on the seat of his bicycle looking very happy only he runs into the protagonist of the film and he falls off his bike. Angry, he gets up and yells at him: 'And you! What do you think you are doing? Do you think you are starting a revolution?'"

I like photographing with natural light. I think it is more flattering and I took photos of his daughter standing by a window. Mostly head shots. They came out well. It was easy, she was so pretty.

My husband liked the photographs as well. Especially one of his daughter. He asked me to enlarge it and frame it for him, which I did.

"The photograph is on my desk in the office," he told me. "And I tell everyone who comes in and admires it that you took it."

"Shall I make copies of these photographs for your mother?" I asked his daughter.

She hesitated. "Sure," she said. "I think Mom would like to have them."

I put a whole bunch of five-by-eight photos of him riding the bicycle and of her standing by the window in a manila envelope and gave them to his daughter. I wrote her name on the envelope, but I never heard back from her.

The time I dropped off his son's book at her apartment and *she* answered the door in her tai chi outfit, *she* was not looking her best. Her hair was caught up in a messy ponytail and I could see the lines on her face. In a way, I was glad to see her looking older and in slight disarray.

At his daughter's wedding, *she* was wearing a beautiful shiny gray—more like silver—silk suit. It was beautifully cut and it looked expensive. When *she* got up to dance with my husband, *she* took off the jacket and, underneath it, *she* was wearing a cream-colored tank top and her arms were bare.

You're just too good to be true
Can't take my eyes off of you

At the dinner party where we first met, my husband had complimented me on my outfit—the black tuxedo trousers with the satin stripe down the side and the white silk blouse. He was friendly and, unlike most men I know, he asked me about myself and what I did. I told him I worked in marketing but had just been laid off—I did not tell him why—and that I was looking for another job.

"Oh," he said. "Maybe I can help."

In the *New York Times*, I read that Seymour Lipkin, the pianist and conductor—her teacher at the Curtis Institute of Music—died on November 16 in Blue Hill, Maine, at the age of eighty-eight. In the obituary, Margalit Fox wrote: "Underpinning Mr. Lipkin's music-making was his intense sense of communion with the works he performed. That communion was often rooted in deeply personal dialogues he held with composers—exchanges that required only Mr. Lipkin to be present.

"In an interview with the *Philadelphia Enquirer* in 2012, he recounted one especially productive conversation:

Beethoven: Lipkin! Make a sforzando here!

Lipkin: Ludwig, I don't feel like it!

Beethoven: Shut up and do what I tell you!

To his credit, and to the plaudits of critics, Mr. Lipkin generally did."

Had *she* heard?
Did *she* read the newspaper? The obituaries?
Should I call and tell her?

There is a video recording on YouTube of Seymour Lipkin playing Chopin's Nocturne in F Sharp Major, Op. 15, No. 2.

Eighty-six years old at the time, Seymour Lipkin played with great tranquility and nobility. His head slightly bent, his body quite still, he performed without ostentation or flamboyance. Once or twice, he put his left hand on his lap while he played with only his right. He made playing the piano look both natural and impossibly difficult.

I watched the video three times and, despite my tin ear, each time I felt transported.

And did *she*, I had to wonder, play the Chopin nocturne?

On a few Saturday afternoons during the fall, while my husband was either out of town or too busy, I used to drive his son to soccer practice. The soccer field was a few miles outside the city and, depending on traffic, it usually took us about forty-five minutes to get there. At first, we did not say much to each other except for my asking the usual questions in an attempt to make friendly conversation:

"What position do you play?"

"Defense."

"Is soccer your favorite sport?"

"No, not really."

"What is your favorite sport?"

"I don't know. I like skiing."

"And what else?" I asked

"I like tennis."

"So do I," I told him.

"Did you watch the U.S. Open?" I also asked.

"Yeah—it was great."

"Who did you want to win? Nadal or Federer?"

"Rafa."

"Oh, I was hoping Federer would win," I said.

"Yeah, I like Roger, too."

"He's so elegant," I said. "But Nadal is so handsome. Handsome like you," I added.

Also an avid tennis player, my husband had a foursome once a week on Thursday mornings early. The foursome never varied and, according to my husband, they had been playing together for nearly fifteen years. The men played at a club located in midtown—the same club where my husband's daughter's wedding reception took place—and since my husband left his racket, sneakers, and tennis whites in a locker there, he went directly from the club to his office after the game, and after, I presume, a shower.

The men my husband played tennis with were named Stan, David, and Herbie. I met Stan and David and they were both nice enough, but I never got to meet Herbie. Herbie was my husband's doubles partner. One time, when Herbie left a message on our answering message saying that something had come up and he could not play tennis on Thursday, I got to hear his voice.

"Where is he from?" I asked my husband.

"He's from Virginia," my husband answered. "Why do you ask?"

"No reason. Just curious," I said.

"I liked his accent," I also said.

"Now we'll have to get the pro to fill in for him on Thursday," my husband said.

Herbie was the name of my landlord before I got married, when I lived in what was called a "railroad flat" in a town house in the East Village. I had moved there before the area became trendy and my rent was relatively cheap and, more important, stabilized. A ground-floor apartment—nothing fancy, but comfortable—that had a bedroom, a good-sized living room, a dining area, and a small serviceable kitchen. But the best thing about it was that it had access to the garden in the back. In the fall, I planted dozens of tulips that bloomed miraculously every spring and I even bought a rickety old secondhand table and a set of plastic chairs to put out there. In the summer, after work, I often invited friends and colleagues to come over—Herbie, too, and his wife, Miranda, came over a couple of times. We had drinks sitting outside and, often too, we ordered Chinese or Thai food and stayed out late. The garden was quiet and peaceful and it did not feel like the city but like country.

Tim looked the same—maybe he had gained a bit of weight—and he still had all his hair. We talked about old times—our misspent youth in New Orleans—and then we caught up.

"I have three kids," Tim told me. "Two are twins. And you?"

I shook my head. "I have two stepkids. And your wife?"

"Amy. She's a nurse practitioner."

"And what brings you to the city?"

"The boat show." Tim laughed. "Didn't I ever tell you that my dream is to sail around the world?"

I shook my head. "Solo?"

"Yes, unless you come with me."

For old times' sake, I told myself.
No regrets.
Sleeping with Tim was familiar.

I tried asking my husband about his old girlfriends—girlfriends before he got married to her. Usually, I would ask after dinner and after we both had had a few glasses of wine and were mellow.

"So who was your first girlfriend?"

"Who did you lose your virginity to?"

My husband laughed, pleased at the attention, pleased to be able to remember.

"The babysitter" he answered. "When I was twelve."

"Twelve? You must be kidding," I said.

"Maybe I was a bit older—thirteen, fourteen."

"What was her name? The babysitter?"

"Rosemary. Rosemary Fitzpatrick. She was Irish."

"A Catholic?"

My husband shrugged.

"And who was next?" I asked.

And during those same evenings after dinner when we both had drunk too many glasses of wine, I also wanted to ask him:

And who do you love best? Me or her? And who fucks best, me or her?

"My beauty" was what my husband sometimes called me—*ma belle!*

In the photo of her pushing the baby carriage down Avenue Foch in Paris, it was hard to tell—even with a magnifying glass—whether *she* looked happy. But my guess was that *she* was not happy. A new baby, a stubborn little dog, a foreign country, a preoccupied husband . . .

The first time I called her—I called her from a phone booth so *she* could not trace the call—*she* picked up right away and I hung up. The second time, the phone rang several times until her voice mail picked up: *Leave a message and I will call you back as soon as I can,* I heard her say.

His son had her nose, the Grecian nose, like Michelangelo's *David.* But aside from that he did not look like her. He was dark and *she* was blond. A good-looking boy and it was probably a mistake to have told him he was handsome. Instead of complimenting him, I had embarrassed him.

"Self-confidence is important," I told my husband in order to justify myself.

And David put his hand in his bag, and took thence a stone, and slang it, and smote the Philistine in his forehead, that the stone sunk into his forehead; and he fell upon his face to the earth.

Happy birthday, stepmother!
I haven't any money to buy you a present, but I'll study hard and be first in my class, and that will be my present. You're the best and the fairest one of all, and I dream of you every night.
Happy birthday again!

Alfonso

On the first page of his novel, *In Praise of the Stepmother*, Mario Vargas Llosa has the devious little stepson write a letter to his stepmother, Lucrecia, on her fortieth birthday.

According to the *Daily Mail*, five years after he won the Nobel Prize in 2010, Mario Vargas Llosa, aged seventy-nine, left Patricia, his wife of fifty years, for former Filipino beauty queen and socialite Isabel Preysler, saying: "I'm done. Now I feel what happiness is. I don't have much time left."

Marina and I worked in the same office and we often shared properties and clients. Instead of getting a job in marketing, I had gotten my real estate license. It was not a job I felt passionate about, but it was a job that gave me some income and some freedom, and where I could meet people. Marina had grown up in the Czech Republic; there she had met, married, and later divorced an American who had brought her to the States. She was young and lively and we became friends. She told stories about how, in Prague as a child, she joined her parents in the demonstrations that led to the Velvet Revolution. She told how her mother was a good friend of Václav Havel's wife, Olga Splichalova, a charismatic and dashing actress, whom Václav Havel married in 1964.

"Olga was the heroine of the Czech Republic. She was an activist and she was tireless. She also founded a charity to help disabled people, especially the elderly and children. It still exists today, " Marina said proudly.

"Have you ever read Václav's *Letters to Olga*—the essays he wrote to her from prison?"

I shook my head.

"She was the most wonderful person I have ever met and I will never forget her," Marina continued.

"Was she beautiful?" I asked.

"She was striking looking but I would not say beautiful. Also, she had lost four fingers in her left hand in an accident—the reason perhaps she was so intent on helping the handicapped."

"What kind of accident?" I asked Marina.

"As a young girl she worked in a factory and she lost her fingers operating a machine."

"Awful," I said, shaking my head again.

"Yes, but that never stopped her. I remember that you hardly noticed her missing fingers. And she never mentioned it. She was a brave woman. Also an understanding one." Marina gave a laugh.

"How do you mean?"

"Václav was a famous womanizer. Olga accepted that. Apparently, when Václav was in prison, she used to joke that at least she knew where he was."

I closed the four fingers of my left hand, leaving out my thumb.

Difficult to imagine.

After Olga Splichalova died in 1996, Václav Havel married Dagmar Veškrnová, an actress, in 1997.

When Marina and I were together, I noticed that I thought about her less often. *She* was not part of our conversation.

All of a sudden, for no apparent reason, I remembered his daughter's husband's uncle's name—Jarvis. An odd name which had reminded me of how, in the movie version of Carson McCullers's *The Member of the Wedding*, Julie Harris, who plays Frankie, the awkward, self-deluded twelve-year-old who plans on joining her older sister and the sister's new husband on their honeymoon, says in that peculiar and distinctive way of hers: "'til this afternoon I didn't have a we, but now after seeing Janice and Jarvis, I suddenly realize that the bride and my brother are the we of me." At the wedding reception, I had mentioned this about the name to his daughter's husband's uncle, but he said he had never seen the movie nor read the book.

My sister Eloise called to tell me that her overweight son got into Yale. Early acceptance, she added.

"Hal Junior wants to study architecture. Lots of famous architects went to Yale," she said, starting to list them, "Eero Saarinen, Norman Foster, Richard Rogers, Charles Gwathmey, Maya Lin, Robert Stern, he's the dean of the school—"

"I know," I interrupted her.

"We'll be coming East in September," she then said.

"Let's make a date for dinner," she continued. "I so enjoyed meeting your husband. Harold, too, sends him his regards."

His daughter went to Harvard and graduated magna cum laude; she also got her MBA there as did her husband, but I did not tell Eloise this.

Ned Rorem, Marion Zarsecsna, Samuel Barber, Lukas Foss, Leonard Bernstein, Peter Serkin, Lang Lang, and Yefim Bronfman were some of the famous alumni of the Curtis Institute of Music in Philadelphia.

(In Philip Roth's novel *The Human Stain,* the narrator describes attending a rehearsal of a Yefim Bronfman concert at Tanglewood:

Then Bronfman appears. Bronfman the brontosaur! Mr. Fortissimo. Enter Bronfman to play Prokofiev at such a pace and with such bravado as to knock my morbidity clear out of the ring. He is conspicuously massive through the upper torso, a force of nature camouflaged in a sweatshirt, somebody who has strolled into the Music Shed out of a circus where he is the strongman and who takes on the piano as a ridiculous challenge to the gargantuan strength he revels in. Yefim Bronfman looks less like the person who is going to play the piano than like the guy who should be moving it. I had never before seen anybody go at a piano like this sturdy little barrel of an unshaven Russian Jew. When he's finished, I thought, they'll have to throw the thing out. He crushes it. He doesn't let that piano conceal a thing. Whatever's in there is going to come out, and come out with its hands in the air. And when it does, everything there out in the open, the last of the last pulsation, he himself gets up and goes, leaving behind him our redemption. With a jaunty wave, he is suddenly gone, and though he takes all his fire off with him like no less a force than Prometheus, our own lives now seem inextinguishable. Nobody is dying, nobody—*not if Bronfman has anything to say about it!*)

Marina and I rode down in the elevator with Philip Roth. We had just shown an apartment that was for sale in the building—apparently Philip Roth owned one in the building as well. He gave Marina and me a brief look of appraisal and Marina smiled at him. For a moment Philip Roth hesitated—Marina was good looking.

"What perfume are you wearing?" Philip Roth asked her.

"Shalimar," Marina answered.

Then, turning away, he ignored us both completely. When the elevator reached the ground floor and the doors opened, he got out first.

"Rude," Marina said.

"Misogynist," I said.

Although I caught only a glimpse of her apartment through the open front door when I delivered her son's book, I remembered it distinctly. It was airy and uncluttered and all white. In fact, it was exactly the kind of apartment I would like to have had instead of one filled with old-fashioned antique dark furniture that belonged to my husband's family. In retrospect, I wished I had accepted her invitation and had gone in for a minute. We might have sat down next to each other on the sofa and chatted about ordinary things—the love affair between Nelson Algren and Simone de Beauvoir.

I'm so pleased your daughter is doing so well at Harvard.

Yes, she seems to like her courses a lot.

Once a month, my husband sent her a check for alimony. I never knew for how much. (I tried looking through his checkbook but the check was sent from his office and from a separate bank account.) I did not ask. After all, it was none of my business. And anyway, where money was concerned, my husband was always generous. Among the many presents he gave me, my favorite was a Burmese sapphire from Tiffany.

"For *ma belle!*"

She, I noticed right away, did not wear rings.

Pianists, I have been told—except perhaps Liberace—rarely wear jewelry when they play.

"Will your mother get married again?" I had asked his daughter.

"No," his daughter answered right away, shaking her head. "I don't think so."

"Does she go out—out with men, I mean?" I persisted.

"She has this one guy, she sees."

"Oh," I said.

"She's known him for a long time. They go on vacations together."

"Where do they go?"

"To the Caribbean mostly, and last year they went to France. To the Dordogne. He rented a castle."

"He must be rich," I said.

His daughter shrugged. "He's nice."

"Is he a musician?"

"No. He's a lawyer. He's older."

Set in the heart of the beautiful Dordogne countryside, the château dates back to the fourteenth century and has remained in the same family all those years. The château sits on a private estate of 200 hectares of lawns, meadows, and woodlands, and is located twenty-five minutes from the market town and capital of the Dordogne, Périgueux.

Périgueux is a particularly charming market town full of amenities that include supermarkets, cafés, bars, and a host of excellent restaurants.

Nearby the town of Les Eyzies-de-Tayac-Sireuil is an archaeologist's paradise with many caves containing prehistoric paintings and deposits.

Surely *she* must have gone to Les Eyzies-de-Tayac-Sireuil, where, in 1868, Louis Lartet, a geologist, discovered five Cro-Magnon skeletons, one of the earliest examples of *Homo sapiens*; and surely, too, *she* must have visited the Musée nationale de Préhistoire dedicated to the history of the Neanderthals.

And, on the way back to the fourteenth-century château, did *she* and the rich lawyer stop off and dine at a Michelin-starred restaurant in Périgueux?

Deux personnes pour dîner à huit heures.

"Do you like foie gras?" I asked his son, as I put some slices I had bought into the refrigerator.

He made a face. "They force-feed the geese, don't they?"

"It's called *gavage*," I said. "We once ran an ad for a poultry farm in upstate New York that made pâtés and first I had to look up all that stuff to make sure they did not force-feed their ducks."

"And did they?"

"Apparently they did. Someone from an animal anticruelty society took an undercover video that showed the workers shoving tubes down the ducks' throats and one of the workers was quoted as saying: 'Sometimes the duck doesn't get up and dies.' We had to remove our ad."

His son laughed, then he said, "I'm seriously considering becoming a vegetarian."

"I hope you are not a vegetarian," I said to Marina, who was having dinner with us, as I handed her a plate of foie gras and toast.

"I've never been to the Czech Republic," my husband was saying to her, "and Prague sounds like a city full of history."

At first, I understood my husband to say to Marina, "Prague is a city full of *mystery*," not "full of history."

In an interview Václav Havel described the censorship imposed on his letters during the three and half years he spent in prison:

"We were allowed to write one four-page letter home a week. It had to be legible, with nothing corrected or crossed out, and there were strict rules about margins and graphic and stylistic devices (we were forbidden, for example, to use quotation marks, to underline words, use foreign expressions, etc.) . . . We could write only about 'family matters.' Humor was banned as well . . . the reason my letters are so deadly serious."

Despite the differences in their backgrounds, Havel was totally dependent on his wife, Olga: "*In Olga, I found exactly what I needed: someone who could respond to my own mental instability, to offer sober criticism of my wilder ideas, provide private support for my public adventures. All my life, I've consulted with her in everything I do. She's usually the first to read whatever I write, and if not, then she's certainly my main authority when it comes to judging it."*[1]

Havel's letter to her from prison dated August 11, 1979:

Dear Olga,

It's Saturday at five o'clock. I've already had supper and I'm drinking juice and wondering what you're doing. Most likely you're sitting in the yard (Václav and Olga owned a farmhouse in Hrádeček)—*with some friends, I hope—drinking coffee and thinking about moving into the kitchen to light the stove and make supper. I have to fill in the details of your life like this because I have no authentic news at all.*

And again from a letter dated November 3, 1979:

We've survived a lot already and we'll survive this too. We each have our own basket of worries and we'll each have to work through it in our own way. Above all, we must support, not depress, each other. I don't underestimate your worries in the least, and in some regards it will be harder for you than for me.

1. From an interview with Karel Hvížďāla, published in Czech in *Dálkovy vyslech* (Purely, Surrey, England: Rozmluvy, 1986).

And from still another letter dated New Year's Eve, 1979:

Dear Olga,

Your visit left me feeling wonderful and I think it was very successful. You looked pretty (!) and it suited you, you radiated serenity, poise and purposeful energy, told me many important things—in short I was exceptionally pleased with you. It seems that this time being a grass widow has been good for you; this temporary emancipation from my domination is allowing you to develop your own identity.

I began a letter to her:

I want to explain what happened. Two weeks after we met at that dinner party you did not go to, your husband came over to my apartment—a railroad apartment I rented in the East Village. He had offered to help me look for another job in marketing and I was grateful. We sat in the garden and he admired the tulips. He said something about how the tulips were amazing and how he felt he was in Holland or someplace, which made me laugh. I also told him how I had planted them all myself. We drank a glass or two of wine, an expensive French Pouilly-Fuissé I had bought especially for the occasion because I assumed—rightly!—he was a wine connoisseur . . . I broke off writing the letter.

On a different subject, I began another letter to her:

I want to explain how on my birthday your son and I drank a bit too much champagne and smoked a little . . . Again, I broke off.

I was fairly certain nothing, or nothing damaging, occurred between his son and me. In any case neither one of us was at fault. Yet I could not help being reminded of Mario Vargas Llosa's novel *In Praise of the Stepmother.* Only, in the novel, things get turned around and the stepson sleeps with his stepmother in order to get rid of her.

I cannot forget how at his son's school graduation, one of his teachers, who must have mistaken me for her on account of our last names, came up to me and said:

"Your son is gifted. I don't say that about many of my students, but your son is truly exceptional. Oh, by the way, my name is Miss Lafferty. I'm the mathematics teacher here."

We shook hands and I started to explain that I was only his stepmother, but she continued and said:

"I've taught at this school for twelve years and I have rarely had a student as intelligent and as intuitive as your son. His comprehension of difficult concepts and theories is quite remarkable. I hope he continues with his studies. It would be a great pity if he didn't."

Fortunately, just then, my husband had waved for me to come over and I said good-bye to Miss Lafferty.

In 1844, Hermann Günther Grassmann published his masterpiece, *Die lineale Ausdehnungslehre, ein neuer Zweig der Mathematik* (*The Theory of Linear Extension, a New Branch of Mathematics*), creating an entirely new subject, linear algebra:

Beginning with a collection of "units" $e_1, e_2, e_3, \ldots,$ he effectively defines the free linear space which they generate; that is to say, he considers formal linear combinations $a_1 e_1 + a_2 e_2 + a_3 e_3 + \ldots$ where the a_1 are real numbers, defines addition and multiplication by real numbers (in what is now the usual way) and formally proves the linear space properties for these operations. . . . He then develops the theory of linear independence in a way which is astonishingly similar to the presentation one finds in modern linear algebra texts. He defines the notions of subspace, linear independence, span, dimension, join and meet of subspaces, and projections of elements onto subspaces.[2]

2. Desmond, Fearnley-Sander, "Hermann Grassmann and the Creation of Linear Algebra," *American Mathematical Monthly* 86(1979): 809–17.

Since his work was either ignored or dismissed during his lifetime, Grassmann turned to another discipline, linguistics.

At dinner Marina told us that the Czech language was a West Slavic language and most closely resembled Slovak, Polish, and Silesian.

"Czech word order is very flexible," she also said.

"Give us an example. Say something in Czech," my husband said.

"*Chci se s tebou taky spát.* I can also say the same thing like this," Marina said laughing. "*Chci s tebou spát taky.*"

"What did you say?" I asked her.

"I said dinner is delicious."

While his daughter was trying on her wedding dress and I was buttoning up the row of tiny silk buttons on the back of the dress, I told her how I had always wanted to go to France and how I was taking French lessons.

"You were born there—right?" I said.

"Yes, but I don't remember anything. We left when I was one year old."

"I saw a photo of your mother pushing you in the baby carriage," I said. "She had a little dog on a leash."

"That was Hector. A wirehaired terrier. We brought him back to the States with us. The most disobedient and stubborn dog in the world, according to my mother," she said.

"I would love to have a dog," I told his daughter.

A little later while I was unbuttoning the row of tiny silk buttons on the back of her wedding dress, his daughter said, "Say something. Say something in French."

"Je t'aime bien."

Another argument my husband and I have had was over my collection of photographs. I was proud of the photos and how I had saved enough money to buy them: a color photo by Harry Callahan of a pink house in Morocco, a Henri Cartier-Bresson of a family on a houseboat on the Seine (the man has his back to the camera and is looking at what appears to be his wife, who is holding a child in her arms), a William Wegman of his dog, Fay, standing on a wooden sawhorse, a photo by André Kertész of some metal chairs in the Luxembourg Garden, and several others—and I wanted to hang them up somewhere. I suggested the dining room instead of the dreary family portraits.

"No way," he said. "Those have been there forever."

"Then how about in the library or in the hall instead of those copies of Piranesi prints?"

"Those aren't copies. They're original prints."

The time my husband came over to my apartment and we drank the expensive Pouilly-Fuissé in the garden before we ended up making love, he had admired the photographs. Instead of hanging them up, I had the framed photos on the floor propped up against the walls—the way I had seen a famous architect's photos displayed in a fashion magazine article—and he had to bend down to get a good look at them.

He wore an expensive-looking tweed jacket and a blue shirt that was open at the collar—on entering the apartment, he had taken off his tie and stuffed it into his jacket pocket—gray slacks, and brown loafers with a high polish.

"I really like this one," he had said, pointing to the Henri Cartier-Bresson photograph, "and I have always wanted to live on a houseboat."

"Me, too," I lied.

The morning I was supposed to meet Marina for breakfast at the new French bakery around the corner from the office, she never showed up. I waited and waited before I finally ordered myself a café au lait and a croissant. Twice, too, I tried calling her, first at home, then on her cell phone, but each time there was no answer.

I have forgotten how, at dinner, we got onto the subject, but, turning to me, Marina had corrected my pronunciation: "duh-VOR-jacque—" she said.

"Dvořák is my favorite composer," she added. "Of course, because he is Czech and as a child I used to play the violin. Badly," she added, smiling.

"What about you?" she asked my husband. "Are you musical?"

"No, not really. But my wife—" He paused, then, looking over at me, he said, "I mean my ex-wife was musical. She played the piano."

Then to lighten the mood, my husband said, "In fourth grade, I played the recorder."

"And who did you sleep with next, after the Irish babysitter?" I asked him one Sunday morning after we had made love.

"Honestly," he answered, still holding me in his arms, "I don't remember."

Then, closing his eyes, he smiled. "You," he said. "I slept with you next."

I remember every man I have ever slept with—good and bad.

After my husband and I first made love and after he left—although it had begun to rain—I went out into the garden and took several photographs of the tulips.

Because I had never planted anything and because I am cautious, I followed the directions to a T:

Plant tulip bulbs in the fall, 6 to 8 weeks before a hard frost is expected

Tulips prefer a site with full or afternoon sun

All tulips dislike excessive moisture. The soil should be well-drained, neutral to slightly acidic

Space bulbs 4 to 6 inches apart

Plant bulbs deep—at least 8 inches, measuring from the base of the bulb

Set the bulb in the hole with the pointy end up

Water bulbs right after planting to trigger their growth

Detained out of town, my husband sent a beautiful assortment of tulips, lilacs, and peonies for my fortieth birthday.

"I am surprised he remembered," his son, who answered the door and brought in the flowers, said. "Usually he forgets everybody's birthday."

"What about your mother's birthday—when is it?" I asked.

Mario Vargas Llosa's novel also begins on the stepmother's fortieth birthday.

Her birthday is March 5 and *she* is a Pisces. Pisces is a Water sign and the ruling planet is Neptune. Neptune is associated with the arts, in particular with music! People born under the sign of Pisces are friendly, selfless, compassionate, and wise.

As for me I am a Gemini, an Air sign, and my ruling planet is Mercury. Mercury is associated with aspects of the mind such as communication, writing, and teaching. People born under the sign of Gemini are inquisitive, sociable, and versatile—often showing two sides of their personality.

Often, too, people born under the sign of Gemini feel that their other half is missing and they look for new friends and mentors.

"We should celebrate!" his son had said that evening.

He did not look like my husband, nor did he look like her. Instead he looked a lot like Rafael Nadal—his thick dark hair, his sturdy limbs.

Bored pushing the big old-fashioned baby carriage down Avenue Foch, exasperated pulling stubborn Hector on the leash, frustrated waiting for her husband to come home late from INSEAD, did *she* have an affair with an elegant, dark-haired Frenchman with a patrician-sounding double name—*Jean-Pierre, Jean-Marc . . . ?*

His daughter, on the other hand, looked exactly like my husband, only she was lovely.

"Happy birthday!" His daughter telephoned me.

"Is Dad there?" she also had said. "Can I speak to him?"

"Your father's flight from Seattle was canceled on account of bad weather," I told her. "He should be home tomorrow."

I didn't want her to be concerned or to think that I was.

His daughter was very intuitive. Like her mother, she was a Pisces.

The boarding pass stub in my husband's coat pocket indicated that he had come not from Seattle but from Chicago's O'Hare International Airport.

"Sorry I missed your birthday," he had said as he walked into the apartment, "and that you were home alone last night."

"I had a good book," I said, not looking at him.

Fortunately, incurious, my husband did not ask me the title of the book or what the book was about. Instead, he asked after his son.

"Is he here?"

From the laundry basket, I sniffed his shirt for the scent of Shalimar.

Along with the story of Alfonso's betrayal, Mario Vargas Llosa included six color illustrations of paintings in *In Praise of the Stepmother,* so as to provide the husband Don Rigoberto and his wife Lucrecia with fantasies during their lovemaking. One painting, *Candaules, King of Lydia, showing his wife to Prime Minister Gyges* by Jacob Jordaens, shows a steatopygous (fat-assed) nude. This painting allows Don Rigoberto to impersonate Candaules and rhapsodize about his wife's buttocks: *Each hemisphere is a carnal paradise; the two of them, separated by a delicate cleft of nearly imperceptible down that vanishes in the forest of intoxicating whiteness, blackness, and silkiness that crowns the firm columns of her thighs . . .*

To celebrate, we had opened a bottle of champagne—*pop!* A 1990 Moët & Chandon Dom Pérignon that my husband kept in the refrigerator for special occasions. We also smoked some pot (I haven't smoked pot since I lived in the rented railroad apartment in the East Village), and we did a few lines of cocaine (I haven't done cocaine since I was a student at Tulane), and we laughed a lot—I don't remember what about—laughed so hard we cried. Afterward, to come down, we each took a Valium.

When I woke up the next morning, his son was gone.

The liquor store was out of the 1990 Dom Pérignon when I went to try to replace it. And, anyway, Ken, the salesman, told me, the champagne would have cost me a small fortune.

I could have bought a bottle of Moet & Chandon Brut Imperial for $49.95, but I didn't. Instead when my husband opened the refrigerator and noticed the champagne gone, I told him I gave it to Margarita to celebrate getting her green card.

"You did what? You gave the housekeeper a two-hundred-dollar bottle of champagne!"

We both lied. *Kif-kif,* as the French say.

Ken, the liquor store salesman, liked to chat with his customers. He liked telling them little-known facts about the bottles of alcohol they were buying.

"Dom Pérignon champagne is supposed to be named after a Benedictine monk named Pierre Pérignon, but the fact of the matter is that sparkling wine—"

"Sorry, Ken," I interrupted, "I have to run."

Frowning, my husband asked Margarita, "Did you enjoy the champagne?"

Turning off the vacuum cleaner, Margarita stared at him for a moment before she opened her mouth to answer.

"*Sí, señor,*" she said.

Margarita knew enough—even if she did not always understand what was being said to her in English—to know that it was best never to contradict her employer and risk being fired.

Like Mario Vargas Llosa, Margarita was from Peru and, like Vargas Llosa, she was born in Arequipa—the second-largest and southernmost city in Peru—but unlike Vargas Llosa, a descendant of wealthy criollos, Margarita was a descendant of poor mestizos.

"One more thing," my husband continued, holding up his hand to keep Margarita from turning on the vacuum again, "when you went into the bedroom to clean this morning were my wife and my son in the bed together?"

Again Margarita said, "*Sí, señor.*"

I admitted we slept in the same bed (my husband's king-size sleigh bed), but we did not sleep together—we did not fuck.

Filing for a divorce in New York State is a tedious affair despite Governor David Paterson's signing no-fault divorce into law on August 15, 2010. And even if the divorce is uncontested, many court forms must be filled out and filed:

Summons with Notice or Summons and Complaint

Affirmation of Regularity (Form UD-5, which requests that your case be put on the calendar)

Affidavit of Plaintiff (Form UD-6)

Three copies of the Note of Issue (Form UD-9)

Findings of Fact/Conclusions of Law (Form UD-10)

Judgment of Divorce (Form UD-11)

Part 130 Certification (Form UD-12)

Affidavit of Defendant (Form UD-7, if your spouse signed and returned it to you)

Certificate of Dissolution of Marriage

Postcard, and USC 111—Divorce and Child Support Summary Form.

If your spouse did not sign and return the affidavit of defendant, then you must also file:

Affidavit of Service (Form UD-3), and

Sworn Statement of Barriers to Remarriage (Form UD-4).

If you and your spouse have children together, then you also have to file the forms related to child support (Forms UD-8, UD-8a, and UD-8b).

When all the forms are completed and brought to the county clerk's office to file and the filing fees have been paid—unless a waiver has been granted based on income—the clerk will submit the papers to the judge and if the judge approves the paperwork, he or she will issue a judgment of divorce.

The railroad apartment in the East Village is no longer available—and, if it was, the rent, no doubt, would be triple or quadruple . . .

And what about those tulips?

Hello!

This time I won't hang up if *she* picks up the phone.

Or if her voice mail picks up—*Leave a message and I will call you back as soon as I can*—

I will leave a message asking her if *she* will play Chopin's Nocturne in F Sharp Major, Op. 15, No. 2 for me.